5-MINUTE
BIBLE STUDIES

for

COUPLES

Randy Hunter

NORTHWESTERN PUBLISHING HOUSE
Milwaukee, Wisconsin

Northwestern Publishing House
N16W23379 Stone Ridge Dr., Waukesha, WI 53188-1109
www.nph.net
© 2022 Northwestern Publishing House
Published 2022
Printed in the United States of America
ISBN 978-0-8100-3018-3
ISBN 978-0-8100-3019-0 (e-book)

22 23 24 25 26 27 28 29 30 31   10 9 8 7 6 5 4 3 2 1

TABLE OF CONTENTS

PREFACE

5-Minute Bible Studies: For Couples brings you three devotional Bible studies per week for a year. Through the devotional studies, God's Word speaks to issues and topics that are important for strengthening the special bond we call marriage. The devotions in this book are gathered under 13 different themes. Each theme is the focus of 12 devotions covering four weeks. Because our growth in knowledge of the Bible and our understanding of how to apply it to our lives and marriages is a gradual process, the themes are revisited each season of the year—spring, summer, fall, and winter—with each week looking at the theme from a slightly different angle.

The logical way to use the book would be simply to read through the devotions in order. However, if you prefer to read all the devotions under a particular theme in order, the Table of Contents will help you find all the devotions under each theme.

Either way, the questions will lead you to think about how to apply God's Word to your own marriage, and the Holy Spirit will work through the Word to bless you.

Communicate With Each Other

Is your marriage healthy? How would you answer that question? Perhaps you might say, "Our marriage isn't perfect. But whose is?" That's an easy answer. But it's not the best answer.

While Jesus was having dinner at Matthew's house, many tax collectors and sinners came and ate with him and his disciples. When the Pharisees saw this, they asked his disciples, "Why does your teacher eat with tax collectors and sinners?" On hearing this, Jesus said, "It is not the healthy who need a doctor, but the sick." MATTHEW 9:10-12

The best response according to Jesus is "No. I'm sick, and so is our marriage." If you disagree, count the hurts you've accumulated in your marriage. Marriage needs a doctor. His name is Jesus. He provides more hope for health than any doctor on earth. Jesus is God who has come to heal the sickness in your soul and in your marriage. You can have a great marriage—not because you will learn practical strategies for a healthy relationship in this book (you will) but because your Savior heals. Healed people can live well; that includes living together well for the rest of your lives. This is the most critical communication in your marriage: Jesus saying, "I have come for you."

- Couple A rates their marital satisfaction above average. Couple B rates their marital satisfaction below average. Together, agree on three reasons it's important for each couple to find ways to talk about their marriage with others.

- Privately, write just two questions you might ask another couple to determine the health of their marriage. Agree on a time when you will compare what you've written and discuss what the questions you've written say about the health of *your* marriage.

Pray that you listen well to Jesus' words to you and give attention to the health of your marriage.

Communicate With Each Other

If you want a plant to thrive, you give it attention. If you want your marriage to thrive, it needs attention too.

Grow in the grace and knowledge of our Lord and Savior Jesus Christ. To him be glory both now and forever! 2 PETER 3:18

Earlier in his letter, Peter warned it's possible to be carried away from Christ. Satan will use anything. So Peter encourages us to *grow.* You have grace, the undeserved love of God. You are saved from your sin by Jesus' work. In the analogy, you are a plant. Grow. Stay healthy. Bear fruit. The Spirit tends to you like a plant with the gospel of Jesus found in his Word and sacraments.

If you want your marriage to thrive, give it attention. Grand getaways and lavish vacations are great for those who can swing them. But if that's all it takes, those privileged to enjoy such things would automatically have better marriages. They don't. How can you? Find ways to give your relationship the attention it needs. Here are three questions to discuss on your next date night (tonight?). These questions should take time; don't rush the conversation. Focus on your feelings for your spouse and your life together.

Don't avoid the second question even though you want to. It might sound like an invitation to an argument, but not if you want to serve your spouse. Wait too long to discuss things that bother you, and you risk apathy or resentment. Those are the opposite of love.

- What did you most enjoy about your marriage relationship today?

- What do you wish you could change about your marriage relationship today?

- How can things be made better for both of you?

Pray that you give your attention to the gospel of Jesus and to meaningful conversations for your marriage.

Communicate With Each Other

Do you strive to be great at knowing your spouse? Are you the expert on your spouse? Do you let your spouse know you?

[Jesus said,] "These people honor me with their lips, but their hearts are far from me." MATTHEW 15:8

Jesus quoted Isaiah to show God has never been honored by the superficial: saying the right thing or standing and sitting at the right time. God knows the heart and seeks the heart. The Christian life is a life of repentance because our hearts are corrupt. God gave you a new heart in Baptism, and he feeds it in the Lord's Supper. That new heart is honest. We talk to God about our deepest need, our need for forgiveness. We hear from him our deepest desire, our desire for absolution. Christians practice self-disclosure every day. We call it repentance: sorrow over sin, trust in God's forgiveness, and commitment to a new life.

You can do this with each other too. You can disclose yourself to your spouse. In marriage, self-disclosure isn't always about confessing your sin. It's about letting your spouse know the person inside you that no one else knows.

The following activities will help you build trust and bring your relationship to a deeper level. They may not be easy at first, but the more you confide in your spouse, the more likely it is that he or she will confide in you. Silence tends to isolate us; self-disclosure tends to connect us.

- Determine one or two hopes or dreams that first belonged to one of you but now you share (e.g., hunting, dancing, camping, business venture, etc.).

- After that conversation, discuss why you think self-disclosure can be difficult and what could make it easier.

Pray that you are honest about your heart, honest with God, and honest with your spouse about your hopes and dreams.

Appreciate Each Other

❖

Do you like it when your spouse appreciates you? Do you think your spouse likes it when you appreciate him or her? What are you doing to show that appreciation to each other?

"The Lord bless you and keep you; the Lord make his face shine on you and be gracious to you; the Lord turn his face toward you and give you peace." NUMBERS 6:24-26

Have you heard of survivor's guilt? An infantryman dies in an ambush, and his sergeant feels guilty for having led his men down that street. Many soldiers feel guilty for returning home when some of their fellow soldiers didn't. Our story should be one of survivor's guilt—but it isn't. We've taken our Lord and each other for granted; our guilt is real. Yet we survive. God has been gracious to you, has turned his face toward you, and has given you peace. You've survived, and your guilt is gone. Now God shows his fondness for you, especially in Jesus.

What are you doing to express your fondness for each other? It's easy to say, "Oh, she knows." What if the Lord had said that about his fondness for you? You wouldn't know. Your spouse needs to know your appreciation. Scan the horizon of your marriage looking for fault and you'll find it. Scan the horizon looking for reasons and ways to express your appreciation for your spouse and you'll find them too.

- In the next 24 hours, both of you commit to asking one other married person, "How does your spouse express appreciation for what you do?" Tomorrow discuss what you've learned.

Pray that you enjoy the Lord's favor without guilt; pray that you find new ways to express your appreciation to each other.

❋ SPRING ❋

Appreciate Each Other

Imagine what a home is like when appreciation is the norm. Maybe yours is like that. Perhaps you can't imagine it. Either way, see the value of pursuing a climate and culture of appreciation.

[Jesus said,] "Just as Moses lifted up the snake in the wilderness, so the Son of Man must be lifted up, that everyone who believes may have eternal life in him." JOHN 3:14,15

When the Israelites failed to appreciate the Lord's care, they faced venomous snakes (Numbers 21). They deserved that death; they did not deserve the Lord's fondness. But the Lord directed Moses to lift up the bronze snake. It was a solution for all to see, to trust, and because of it, to live. Our failure to trust in the Lord's care deserves death too. He's provided a similar but better solution for us: Jesus lifted up for all to see, to believe, and through him, to live.

The marriage you're building shows your appreciation for the Lord's fondness for you and your spouse. It's your home. You're the only ones who can make it a more appreciative place.

- In two minutes, list as many things as you can that remind you of the Lord's fondness for you. The one with the longer list gets to name the prize!

- Tell each other *(a) one specific situation* when you felt appreciated by your spouse and *(b) one specific situation* when you felt unappreciated. It would be easy to get defensive, but you don't have to. You can just listen, learn, and thank. The point isn't to hurt. The point is to be honest about what you're feeling. You can't argue with that.

Pray that you take to heart what your spouse tells you about when he or she feels unappreciated, asking God to give you the words and actions that will build a culture of appreciation in your home.

❈ SPRING ❈

Appreciate Each Other

Does your spouse know how often you think of him or her? How often does your spouse hear you say, "I respect you" or "I love you"? Find ways to let your spouse know and use your words to communicate love and respect even when it's hard—especially when it's hard.

Each one of you also must love his wife as he loves himself, and the wife must respect her husband. EPHESIANS 5:33

Your spouse may drive you crazy some days, but deep down, you know this is someone Jesus cares for and loves. According to the apostle Paul's words above, that's enough to make your spouse worthy of your respect and honor.

Research has suggested that in good marriages husbands and wives have five times more positive interactions than negative ones. That means that if you said something unkind to your spouse or neglected to show appreciation to him or her but thought you were making up for it by saying something kind or showing appreciation, you're running an 80 percent deficit! You're not breaking even; you're way behind.

For each of the following statements, determine if it's *(a)* true and your spouse knows it or *(b)* not true and what actions you can do to change it.

1. I can easily list three things I admire about my spouse.

2. When we are apart, I often think fondly of him or her.

3. I look for ways to tell my spouse "I love you."

4. My spouse enjoys my accomplishments.

5. My spouse usually appreciates the things I do in this marriage.

Pray that you see your spouse as someone loved and cared for by Jesus, and pray that you find ways to show your appreciation for him or her.

Manage Conflict

❖

Have you ever been in a conflict about something that seemed trivial but ended up being serious? Did you later realize that you had equated the cause and content of the conflict, only to discover later that they were different?

[Adam] said, "The woman you put here with me— she gave me some fruit from the tree, and I ate it." GENESIS 3:12

Adam is every man and woman. When God confronted Adam with his sin, Adam thought the cause of his conflict with Eve was her action. He learned that was only the content, not the cause. The actual cause of their conflict was his heart. He was with Eve when Satan came calling, but instead of sending a warning, he extended his hand and took the fruit. God told them the ugly consequences of their sin and made equally clear his beautiful grace in the promise of an offspring of the woman who would crush the serpent's head.

We play out that same pattern in our living rooms and kitchens when we mistake the content for the cause. Even the most trivial matter can quickly escalate into something significant and hurtful. When you're itching for a fight, it's easy to find one.

- Identify the content (what it looks like it's about) and the cause (what it's really about) of this conflict.
  "The Browns want us to come for dinner on Saturday."
  "No, I'm tired. Let's not."
  "You're tired? But today is Tuesday. Are you saying you'll be tired Saturday?"
  "I'm saying I'm tired of going out. I just want to stay home and relax."
  "How about what I want to do?"
  "You always want to go out. And we go out a lot."
  "Your idea of a lot and my idea of a lot are quite different."
  "No kidding! Just look at our sex life."

- Tell each other what you learned from this activity—other than it's easy when it's someone else's conflict!

Pray that you confess the sin in your heart in any conflict and get to the cause, not just the content.

❋ SPRING ❋

Manage Conflict

The best way to manage conflict is to prevent it. How's that working for you?

The Lᴏʀᴅ is my shepherd, I lack nothing. PSALM 23:1

Do you believe that? David knew much about his Savior but not as much as you know. You have Jesus' entire life and ministry in the four gospels. Yet David could say that because of his Lord's mercy and provision, he lacked nothing. That's faith. That's what it sounds like when you find your identity in Christ.

When your identity is wrapped up in who you are because of Christ and his care for you, you can say and do things that prevent conflict. You can know when you're feeling deprived in your marriage and say it. You can speak what it is you feel like you're missing. You can listen to your spouse and show empathy without getting defensive. If you can do that, you can prevent ___ percent of your conflicts (fill in the blank however you wish).

So many conflicts come from feeling deprived of something. Of what?

- Privately make a list of five possible things a husband or wife could feel deprived of. When you're done, compare your lists and explain your items.

- You lack nothing because you are in Christ. That's your identity. With that in mind, tell each other one thing you would like more or less of in your marriage.

- As you listen to your spouse tell you what he or she would like more or less of, remember your identity in Christ. Show empathy. Ask questions. Resist being defensive. Listen to understand, not necessarily to agree.

Pray that you find your identity not in things or abilities but in Christ and that you can be quick to listen to what your spouse would like more or less of.

❄ SPRING ❄

Manage Conflict

Every conflict in your marriage presents a choice. You'll either withdraw, argue to protect yourself, or reach out and better understand your spouse.

I urge you to live a life worthy of the calling you have received. Be completely humble and gentle; be patient, bearing with one another in love. EPHESIANS 4:1,2

Our consciences testify we have a conflict with God. But Paul reminds us we are in Christ because God called us. He chose to give us credit for his Son's righteousness and call us his children. Because he has removed the conflict of sin, we can bear "with one another in love." Make allowances for each other's faults because of God's love for you and the love you can show your spouse.

Sometimes the best we can do is just to put up with each other. It's not very romantic, but it's honest. But sometimes we can do better. We can choose to reach out and better understand each other. Here are ten things you can say when you have a conflict. Determine if each one is either *(a)* withdrawing and arguing to protect yourself or *(b)* reaching out and learning to better understand your spouse.

1. You always have to be right.
2. This must be hard for you.
3. Tell me more.
4. You never care how I feel.
5. How can you think that?
6. I didn't know you felt that way.
7. There you go again; same old, same old.
8. I'm so sorry I hurt you when I said that.
9. That's the dumbest thing I've ever heard.
10. I want to understand how you feel.

Pray that God would help you respond to your spouse in ways that show you want to bear "with one another in love."

Serve Each Other

Tell each other about an occasion in your marriage when you felt honored by your spouse.

Greater love has no one than this: to lay down one's life for one's friends. JOHN 15:13

True love is using all that you are and have to benefit someone else. That accurately describes what Jesus has done for the world, doesn't it? We are self-serving at the core, but Jesus, at his core, is committed to serving others. He served you to the point of laying down his life so you could go through life knowing he calls you friend.

Jesus' selfless service to me changes me. I can get over my selfish serving of myself and use what I have and who I am to serve my spouse. I won't do it perfectly. I'll need daily reminding and forgiveness, but that's what God's grace does.

That time when you felt honored by your spouse—I'd guess it was a time when your spouse *did* something for you. It was not simply a thought, but your spouse *acted* on it to serve you, to put you and your happiness first.

You only have a life with God because Jesus did that for you. Imagine the kind of marriage you'd have if that's what you would do for each other.

Go back to those occasions you discussed earlier. Tell each other:

- If you were the doer: What made you do that? How did you feel when you did that? Were you aware of how much it meant to your spouse?

- If you were the receiver: How did you feel when it happened? Have you told anyone about it? Even now, when you think about it, what happens?

Pray that you learn to serve each other.

❉ SPRING ❉

Serve Each Other

How do you divide the chores in your house? The way your parents did? By your interest or skill? By traditional man or woman roles?

Now to each one the manifestation of the Spirit is given for the common good. 1 CORINTHIANS 12:7

The Holy Spirit shows up in every believer with different gifts. He gives spiritual gifts, natural abilities, and personality traits but always "for the common good."

How are you using your abilities to best divide the load of caring for your household? Just because one of you started doing the laundry 2 years ago or 20 years ago doesn't mean it has to stay that way. Or maybe your spouse just has the gift of cleaning out the cat's litter box, and he or she really wants to do that. But maybe not. Perhaps it's time to talk about who is doing what.

Research shows that nearly three-quarters of married women are dissatisfied with their roles in household management while only a quarter of men feel that way. Those are just statistics. What matters is how your spouse feels about it.

You must be brave and honest to do this next activity; you also must be willing to adjust. Get ready by immersing yourself in the gospel: what Jesus has done to serve you, how he made himself nothing to serve you. Then you're prepared to have an honest conversation about who does what in your household.

- Work together to create two lists: (1) the chores he does to keep your household in order and (2) the chores she does to keep your household in order.

- Ask yourself and each other, "Are you satisfied with what you see?"

Pray that you have the grace to want to serve your spouse and the wisdom to adjust where it will help.

Serve Each Other

❖

What makes your spouse say, "I know you are committed to me"?

**Hope deferred makes the heart sick,
but a longing fulfilled is a tree of life.** PROVERBS 13:12

Hope is confident expectation. We sing, "In Christ alone my hope is found." Our confident expectation is that Christ has paid for our sin and reconciled us with God. The Holy Spirit has no interest in deferring that hope. He wants to pour it into every soul.

What does your spouse hope for in your marriage? Hope deferred makes the heart sick—literally, worn out as if rubbed away. Unmet expectations wear a person out. On the other hand, fulfill your spouse's longing, and your marriage looks like a healthy tree.

How do you find out what your spouse hopes for in your marriage? Be honest and courageous enough to ask, answer, and listen. If you say, "Oh, I don't know," you get what you deserve. But have the courage to pursue the conversation below and enjoy a tree of life.

- Write one expectation you long for in your relationship and one way your spouse could help meet it. Write it down so you get it right. Be realistic; your spouse may never be your partner on *Dancing with the Stars*. Then think about it for a week before the two of you tell each other what you've written.

- When you tell your spouse, the goal is not to demand or even negotiate, just to communicate. When you listen to your spouse, the goal is not to crush, correct, or agree but to honor his or her expectation.

Pray that you can honestly and kindly tell your spouse what you hope for in your marriage. Pray that you can hear what your spouse's hope is and joyfully fulfill it.

Spiritual Intimacy

God had in mind the gospel when he instituted marriage, and then he used marriage to help us understand the gospel. But how?

Be filled with the Spirit, speaking to one another with psalms, hymns, and songs from the Spirit. Sing and make music from your heart to the Lord, always giving thanks to God the Father for everything, in the name of our Lord Jesus Christ. Submit to one another out of reverence for Christ. EPHESIANS 5:18-21

Certain actions show you're filled with the Spirit: speaking and singing Scripture and giving thanks. Then Paul adds one more: submitting, i.e., willingly putting others ahead of yourself. It's what Christ-followers do because it is what Christ did for us. Only when the Spirit moves you to submit, to put your spouse and your spouse's happiness ahead of your own, will you be able to face the challenges of marriage with grace.

Marriage isn't always a smile-fest, and when it isn't, you know where to go for fuel. If your only source of love and grace is your spouse, then when he or she isn't filling you up, it's devastating. Your spouse can't fill your tank the way the Spirit can. To look for it is to seek the impossible. But the Spirit, working through the means of grace, the gospel in Word and sacrament, fills your life with so much grace you can give love and kindness to your spouse even if he or she isn't filling you up at the moment. The gospel is what our hearts were made to run on.

- When in your life did you feel closest to God? Tell each other and make a plan to get back there.

Pray that you are filled with the Spirit through the gospel and that it shows in how you put your spouse first.

❋ SPRING ❋

Spiritual Intimacy

Summarize these verses in one word:

If you have any encouragement from being united with Christ, if any comfort from his love, if any common sharing in the Spirit, if any tenderness and compassion, then make my joy complete by being like-minded, having the same love, being one in spirit and of one mind. Do nothing out of selfish ambition or vain conceit. Rather, in humility value others above yourselves, not looking to your own interests but each of you to the interests of the others. PHILIPPIANS 2:1-4

How about the word *serve?* Paul starts with our union with Christ: buried with him and raised with him. Baptized into him, you now are inseparable from him. When the Spirit drives that good news deep into our hearts, it changes us, and we can serve one another.

Marriage is different from our other relationships because it's so daily. Every few minutes, we have to decide, *Am I going to serve my spouse gladly, or will I coldly and selfishly insist on my own way?* So when your spouse asks after getting into bed, "Did I blow out the candle in the den?" she's really asking, "Will you serve me?" And you get to decide.

In that moment, you're living out the gospel. You're changed by how Jesus has served you, and you want to serve your spouse. Yes, blowing out a candle can show spiritual intimacy. So can doing the dishes or filling up the car. Sacrifice for your spouse in little or big ways, and you're showing your union with Christ.

- Fill in the blank: "One way I may have been thinking of myself more than you lately is _____. And I'd like to change that."

Pray that your union with Christ unites you all the more to each other.

❊ SPRING ❊

Spiritual Intimacy

The Christian response to Christ is not to think less of yourself but to think of yourself less. Paul gave a reason for putting your spouse ahead of yourself.

Submit to one another out of reverence for Christ. EPHESIANS 5:21

The old King James Version translated this verse, "Submitting yourselves one to another in the fear of God." Some translations today stick with *fear* because that's the word, but there's a kind of fear that's terror and a kind that's awe. Fear is the natural reaction of being in the presence of something or someone greater than yourself. Terror is knowing God as judge. Awe is knowing God as Savior. One is law, the other gospel. Either way, when you encounter God, your knees begin to shake. He's the one at work in you.

Sometimes married people know each other so well they can finish each other's sentences. They just know how the other thinks and feels. How would your marriage be different if you so immersed yourself in the words and promises of Jesus that when you faced a challenge, Jesus' words came out?

You'd look at your spouse differently. You'd think of your marriage as sacred. You'd take complaints without being crushed because you know who you are in Christ. You'd voice complaints with gentleness and kindness because Jesus is in you.

The only way to avoid sacrificing your spouse on the altar of your own selfishness is to see the One who loves you like no other. Filled with his love, you can genuinely love and serve your spouse in the fear of God.

- Privately write two things your spouse does to serve you. When you're done, tell each other.

Pray that you think less of yourself and more of your spouse.

15

Get On the Same Page With Your Finances

The belief that your spouse spends money foolishly is a leading contributor to divorce. Conflicts over money matter. Would you like to get on the same page about money?

"You cannot serve both God and money." MATTHEW 6:24

Isn't that an interesting turn of the phrase? We usually think, *I want more money so that I can be served by it.* But Jesus said there are two options: You serve God, or you serve money.

How can you tell which one you're serving? Probably by how much you think about each and what motivates your decisions about them. Money is a tool from God for us to use to achieve his goals for our lives. When you're married, one of his goals is that you use your money to serve each other. That means getting on the same page with your finances. The following activities will help.

Without showing your spouse, write how much money you can spend without talking about it together first. Do it right now, then show your spouse.

Surprised? You've started an important conversation about money. Now continue it.

- Privately: Determine three financial goals you'd like to reach in the next six months and three financial goals you'd like to attain in the next five years. Write all six goals on a piece of paper, but don't show each other until you're both done.

- Together: Compare what you've written. Ask questions. Try to understand your spouse, not convince him or her. Take your time. That's how we serve each other and put the other first.

Pray that the Lord gives us unity and patience while we work to get on the same page with our finances.

Get On the Same Page With Your Finances

Have you ever bought something and wondered, Who has that $20 bill now? *You used it, but it's not gone.* Whose is it now?

> **Yours, LORD, is the greatness and the power and the glory and the majesty and the splendor, for everything in heaven and earth is yours. . . . Wealth and honor come from you.**
> 1 CHRONICLES 29:11,12

In a way, your money is yours, but in a much bigger way the Bible says it belongs to God. It came from him, it's his, and it's going back to him.

You'll only hear that from God's Word and his people. This world, our own fallen reasoning, and Satan himself want us to believe it's ours to do with as we please. In a marriage, two fallen people will likely disagree on what pleases them about money. Just as the Spirit gets us on the same page with our trust in Jesus, he can get us on the same page with our view of money.

The Spirit convinces us money is tricky. Jesus told a story about a person who heard the truth of God's love but "the deceitfulness of wealth choke[d] the word, making it unfruitful" (Matthew 13:22). Money isn't bad by nature. It is a tool, and like any tool it can be used well or poorly, for good or bad. Jesus wants us to know money can be like the deceitful serpent in the Garden of Eden. We spend a good deal of time thinking about, working for, and dreaming of what Jesus calls deceitful. To get on the same page with our finances, look the monster in the eyes.

- Individually write three ways money can be deceitful. When you're done, tell each other and create a list. Maybe put it on your refrigerator. It could be quite a conversation starter when guests read it.

Pray that you remember whose money you have.

Get On the Same Page With Your Finances

Do you track your spending to the penny or just spend till the money's gone? Does Jesus keep track of our money?

"The Son of Man is going to come in his Father's glory with his angels, and then he will reward each person according to what they have done." MATTHEW 16:27

Jesus says something similar at the end of Revelation, again referring to his return at the end of the world: "My reward is with me, and I will give to each person according to what they have done" (22:12). In both verses, the word Jesus used for "reward" could be translated "paycheck." Grace still prevails. Grace means he gives us what we don't deserve, but he keeps track of our obedience too. Some suggest we think in terms of rewards of grace, gifts he gives because he loves us.

We like to put our lives into boxes. There's the politics box, the church box, the sex box, the money box, etc. We may see it that way, but God doesn't. You and everything in your life are in one box. What might change if we saw things God's way?

1. What others think of us wouldn't matter so much. Maybe we'd spend less money trying to impress people with things we don't need.

2. We'd filter our purchases differently. Maybe we'd find ourselves asking, "Will this bring glory to God and joy to me, or will it be a blessing to others?"

3. We'd find our value in who we are, not in what we have. Maybe we'd more easily rejoice with those who have more than we have and share with those who have less than we have.

- Which of the three items above hits home for you? Explain your reasons to each other.

Pray that you would see your money as Jesus does.

❀ SPRING ❀

Know Each Other

Quick: Name your spouse's best friend (other than you) and one thing your spouse wants to accomplish in the next year. You're starting where you are now, but you can get to know each other better.

"They will all know me, from the least of them to the greatest," declares the LORD. "For I will forgive their wickedness and will remember their sins no more." JEREMIAH 31:34

Our Lord uses human experiences to help us understand who he is and what he does. It's all we know. He gives us his law, so we know what wickedness is. He promises to forgive wickedness, so we know what grace is. Or better, so we know *him*. God wants you to know him as the one who forgives your sin. We can never know him too well.

The way you know each other is a little picture of knowing God. You're never done knowing God better. And a husband and wife are never done knowing each other better. If this is a strong suit for you, praise God! Your detailed information about each other will help you build your marriage. If this is a weakness for you, if too much time has passed with too little openness about your everyday life, hopes, fears, and dreams, praise God! You know God's grace and forgiveness for past failures. And you're working on knowing each other better.

- Try to name each other's top three current stresses, top two current aspirations, and basic philosophy of life.

- Find out your spouse's favorite book and read it!

Pray that you enjoy what it means to *know* the Lord and that you let that joy move you to find ways to better know your spouse.

Know Each Other

There was a time you didn't know each other. Whether you've been married 1 month or 50 years, you're still getting to know each other. How's that going? You'll never arrive, but you can move toward knowing each other better. There also was a time you didn't know God.

Once you were not a people, but now you are the people of God; once you had not received mercy, but now you have received mercy. 1 PETER 2:10

Peter takes us back to the way we were by nature. We were all born without faith in Jesus; God's mercy was out there, but it wasn't mine. The Holy Spirit worked through his powerful Word connected to the water in Baptism to change that. I became one of God's people. Mercy wasn't just out there; it was and is mine. The rest of my life is my time to grow to better know this God who made me one of his and showed me mercy.

Just like there are advantages to knowing God better, there are advantages to knowing each other better. Don't settle for less!

- Privately record your answers to the questions below and then tell each other.

  My spouse's favorite hobby is . . .

  Two of my spouse's closest friends are . . .

  My spouse's favorite TV show is . . .

  Two of my spouse's favorite foods are . . .

  A spiritual goal of my spouse is . . .

- Together, create a list of benefits that you have found from knowing God better.

Pray that you get to know God better through meditation on his Word and that you get to know each other better, no matter how long you've been married.

❋ SPRING ❋

Know Each Other

Have you ever wondered how much of life you've missed because you weren't paying attention? How many tender moments with each other never happened because you were wrapped up in something else? How many beautiful scenes you never saw because you were looking down at your phone?

If a man has recently married, he must not be sent to war or have any other duty laid on him. For one year he is to be free to stay at home and bring happiness to the wife he has married. DEUTERONOMY 24:5

That's some powerful incentive to get married! It might even make you long for theocracy—that time when God was king in Israel. This verse appears without comment; no rationale is given. But you can imagine possible reasons for it: to demonstrate the value of marriage, teach Israel the commitment of marriage, and help newlyweds start and set a pattern for knowing each other. The Lord was teaching married people to pay attention to each other.

When we were young, our parents and teachers told us to pay attention. Now it's up to us. How well are you paying attention to each other?

How would a spouse who *isn't* paying attention answer the following questions? Have some fun with this!

- What is your spouse's favorite hobby?

- Who are two of your spouse's closest friends?

- What is your spouse's favorite TV show?

- What are two of your spouse's favorite foods?

- What is a spiritual goal of your spouse?

You may not have gotten a year off to get to know each other, but you do have the gift of marriage and your time together. Don't waste it. Get to know each other.

Pray that you pay more careful attention to your spouse.

Connect With Each Other

❖

Do you like it when your spouse notices what you do and thanks you for it? Of course you do! Your spouse feels the same way. When that happens, you build a connection with each other. When Paul was closing his letter to the Romans, he singled out dozens of people and complimented them.

Greet Mary, who worked very hard for you. ROMANS 16:6

What do you think Mary did? Maybe she handled logistics for his travels. Perhaps she made sure Paul had a hot meal when he was in town. The possibilities are endless. We have no idea, but Paul did, and he wanted everyone to know that she worked hard.

This was the same Paul who wrote, "I know that good itself does not dwell in me, that is, in my sinful nature" (Romans 7:18). He wasn't confused. Paul was not implying that somehow Mary's righteousness earned God's favor. Her righteousness came from Christ. She was just living in response to it, and Paul was complimenting her for it.

Consider developing a habit of giving your spouse at least one compliment a day for the rest of your life. How long would it take you to develop that habit? Developing a new habit takes one to two months. So if you split the difference, you could think of a month and a half. Oh, and let's add a twist. Make sure at least once a week it's a compliment your spouse has never heard before. Game on?

- Recall the last compliment you heard from your spouse. Tell each other and describe how it made you feel.

- Discuss what it would take to do the One-a-Day Compliment plan.

Pray that you would be more complimentary of others, especially your spouse.

Connect With Each Other

Your spouse wants to feel connected to you. One of the best ways to get and keep that feeling of being connected is to take time for each other. God created time and uses it for his glory to help us know him.

God called the light "day," and the darkness he called "night." And there was evening, and there was morning—the first day. GENESIS 1:5

God exists outside of time, but he made promises of a Savior in time. When that time had fully come, God sent his Son. Jesus told his disciples to work while it is day. And he has set a day when he will judge the world. God is all about time, not because he needs it but because you do. You need time to come to faith in him and live for him. That's how we give God glory.

Have you thought of your marriage as your vehicle to glorify God? It is. You glorify him when you take the time to build your connection with each other. If you don't give each other time, you will become disconnected. Nobody wants that, especially not the God who gives you time.

- Make a list of things you agree are "time suckers." These aren't necessarily bad things, just optional activities that rob you of time you could spend together.

- Make another list of things you agree are "time savers." These are things that work in your favor, that help you spend time together.

- Tell each other your observations about these two lists.

Pray that you acknowledge time as God's gift, that you find ways to take time for each other, and that you eliminate some things that rob you of time with each other.

Connect With Each Other

When a person gives you time and attention, you feel connected, whether that person is a store clerk or your spouse. When our Lord gives us his time and attention, we call it fellowship.

Our fellowship is with the Father and with his Son, Jesus Christ. 1 JOHN 1:3

Fellowship means a sharing, a joining together, a connection. Our connection with God doesn't start with us. It starts with God's gift of repentance: We confess our sin and trust Jesus, who gave us more than 30 years of his time and the attention we needed to be declared "not guilty."

John also wrote, "We have fellowship with one another" (1 John 1:7). "Fellowship" is more than coffee and doughnuts after worship. It's our shared condition of needing grace and receiving it by faith in Jesus.

Build your connection by giving each other your time and attention. Talking about how you spend your time can be as dangerous as talking about how you spend money. For this to work, don't blame your spouse or try to figure him or her out. It's not your job to analyze why he spends time on that, or why she spends time on this. Instead, have an honest conversation about how you spend your time.

- When do we go to bed? When do we get up?

- How often do we go out together, just the two of us? Stay home together, just the two of us?

- How much time do we spend with friends? With children? On hobbies?

- How much time do I spend relaxing? Sleeping? Exercising? With God's Word and in prayer?

- How would I like to see our use of time change?

Pray that you would thank God for his time and attention to you and that you would use your time to build your connection with each other.

 **❋ SPRING ❋**

Enjoy Sexual Intimacy

We're all missionaries, even if it's just for our favorite phone or car. We're all missionaries for Christ, even if we don't get on a plane to do it. Could we, Christian married couples, become missionaries for sexual wholeness in marriage?

Let him kiss me with the kisses of his mouth—for your love is more delightful than wine. Pleasing is the fragrance of your perfumes; your name is like perfume poured out. No wonder the young women love you! Take me away with you—let us hurry! Let the king bring me into his chambers. SONG OF SONGS 1:2-4

When most people think of sex and the Bible, they see a wagging finger saying no. The church is to blame for some of that. The church taught for centuries, "There is no marriage and therefore no sex in heaven. Since our time on earth is to prepare us for heaven, our time here is better spent in disciplining ourselves to not need it. Sex is only for having children." See the scolding finger? But that's not in the Bible. Instead of a prudish list of prohibitions, the Bible portrays sex as a passionate path to fulfill what God put in your heart.

God's design for sexuality *includes* passionate sensuality. Count the senses in the verses above. God gave us five senses for many reasons, but when it comes to sexual intimacy, no sense is off-limits if it doesn't hurt the conscience or body of the other and both are willing.

Tell each other what one thing about each sense heightens your sexual arousal for the other:

1. Touch

2. Taste

3. Sight

4. Smell

5. Hearing

Pray that you help each other enjoy passionate sensuality and sexuality as gifts from God.

Enjoy Sexual Intimacy

Our heavenly Father is the perfect parent. Let's learn from him.

Marriage should be honored by all, and the marriage bed kept pure, for God will judge the adulterer and all the sexually immoral. HEBREWS 13:4

When it comes to sex, our heavenly Father provides clear and firm boundaries. God's design for healthy sexuality is restricted to marriage. Our culture doesn't like boundaries of any kind: "I'll decide for myself what I want." But sexuality is so precious God put boundaries around it to protect it. "Enjoy my gift," he says, "within your marriage." He gives hope for the future. Jesus lived in those boundaries for us and credits us with his purity. We're forgiven. He teaches the truth. We don't have to give in to our culture. We can follow his plan for sex and sexuality.

Christian parents follow the same pattern. If God has given you children, provide clear boundaries: "Sex is a beautiful gift of God for you to enjoy when you're married." Project hope for their future: "Your baptism assures you of God's grace when you stumble." Teach the truth: "The Spirit gives us all we need to honor his gift of sex and marriage."

If God has given you children, you are the best people to teach them God's design for sex and sexuality. Sound Lutheran books are available to help you.

Our culture contradicts God's plan for sex. Fear not. Believe the truth. Teach the truth. Even if you bear some negative consequences now, in the end, God wins. You will too.

- Discuss how you learned God's plan for sex in marriage and, if you have children, how you plan to teach them.

Pray that you endeavor to show and tell God's plan for sex in marriage.

Enjoy Sexual Intimacy

Does reading the Bible embarrass you? How about these verses?

May your fountain be blessed, and may you rejoice in the wife of your youth. A loving doe, a graceful deer—may her breasts satisfy you always, may you ever be intoxicated with her love.
PROVERBS 5:18,19

When a famous Christian teacher has been teaching one thing about sexuality but is found out to have been leading a different life, people get the message that Christians must repress their sexuality or they're just hypocrites. Neither is necessary.

God gives firm boundaries for sex. Honor marriage and guard the sanctity of sex between you. God draws a firm line against sex outside of marriage. Jesus offers hope by his pure life and then gives us credit for it. Your past sins don't define you. The Spirit teaches us the truth about his plan for marriage in words like these from Proverbs.

Faith doesn't take away the desire for food, but it keeps us from gluttony. Faith doesn't take away the desire to sleep, but it keeps us from laziness. Faith doesn't take away sexual desire, but it keeps it within God's boundaries. Sexual desire in marriage isn't sinful. God is the one who designed the neural pathways responsible for sexual pleasure. You're not sinning or undisciplined if you get comfortable with that. It's okay to have erotic desires within the boundaries God has designed.

- Were you given the impression growing up that sex is dirty? Reading Song of Songs might correct that.

- Were you given the impression growing up that the only boundary around sex is that it's consensual and you use protection? Discuss reasons why God's plan is better.

Pray that you continue or learn to enjoy God's plan for sexuality in your marriage.

❋ SPRING ❋

Forgive Each Other

Newton's third law of motion states that for every action, there is an equal and opposite reaction. Hurt is like that too. For every hurt, the sinful nature seeks an equal and opposite hurt. Have you heard someone say, "I don't get mad, I get even"? You could write a history of the world on that. Don't make it the history of your marriage.

Three days later, while all of them were still in pain, two of Jacob's sons, Simeon and Levi, Dinah's brothers, took their swords and attacked the unsuspecting city, killing every male. GENESIS 34:25

Shechem raped Jacob's daughter Dinah and then, in true predatory fashion, begged to marry her. Dinah's brothers concocted a ruse to get revenge. They would agree to the marriage if the men of Shechem's tribe were circumcised. When all the men were physically compromised, Dinah's brothers attacked, killed them all, stole their possessions, and took their families as slaves. This sinful example from the Bible proves the point: For every hurt received, the sinful nature seeks to deliver an equal or greater hurt.

The opposite is to forgive. It's the heart of God for you. Imagine where you'd be without it. But don't imagine it for long; simply receive and enjoy it. And show it. You can't live with a sinner, like you do, without needing to forgive and be forgiven. It interrupts the cycle of repaying hurt for hurt.

- Recall two Bible stories that illustrate "for every hurt, people seek an equal and opposite hurt."

- When someone hurts you, do you first get angry or sad?

- Tell each other what has helped you forgive instead of getting even.

Pray that you see the "hurt for hurt" principle in your heart. Then ask God to remove that principle and replace it with his heart of forgiveness.

Forgive Each Other

It usually starts with something unintentional. Your spouse did something that offended you. You're hurt. If it continues, your hurt turns to anger. Your anger leads you to do something or withhold something that offends your spouse. Then your spouse is hurt. See the cycle? How do you break the cycle of offense-hurt-anger-offense-hurt-anger and on and on? It starts here:

He has rescued us from the dominion of darkness and brought us into the kingdom of the Son he loves, in whom we have redemption, the forgiveness of sins. COLOSSIANS 1:13,14

God has forgiven you. That doesn't excuse your spouse's offense against you or make your hurt less real. It just means God has forgiven you for your offenses against him. Sit with that reality and let the Spirit teach you how to forgive.

The Spirit inspired the biblical writers to use different word pictures for forgiveness. There's the Hebrew picture of a scapegoat, led into the wilderness after receiving the people's sins. The scapegoat never comes back. Then there's the image of skipping calves released from the stall and leaping for joy. That's what happens when the burden of sin is removed. The word picture for grace is unconditional love. Something for something is a purchase. Something for nothing is grace.

Let's bring this into your home. Complete the following sentences in your own words and then compare them with each other.

- For us, to forgive each other means . . .

- For us, to forgive each other does not mean . . .

Pray that you become more aware of the depth of the Bible's teaching on forgiveness and that you catch the cycle of offense-hurt-anger in your marriage and replace it with forgiveness.

Forgive Each Other

❖

"I can't forgive him. If I do, it will make it look like it was okay." That's one myth about forgiving someone. There are more. But first, a myth-buster:

If we confess our sins, he is faithful and just and will forgive us our sins and purify us from all unrighteousness. 1 JOHN 1:9

Have you ever thought of the risk God took in forgiving sinners like us? We could see it as a license to do what we want (myth), or that my sin doesn't matter that much (myth), or that God ignores my sin (myth). He knew the myths we would construct around the sacrificial gift of his Son for our forgiveness. He knew we could take advantage of his grace. And he forgave. Hallelujah! What a Savior!

You will never be able to forgive in the same way that God has forgiven you. But don't let that stop you from trying. To see the truth about forgiveness, see through the myths of forgiveness. Determine what's false about each of these myths; use your own words to replace it with the truth.

- When I forgive, I must also forget. (Maybe you shouldn't.)

- The hurt is too great; it's impossible to forgive. (Tell that to the parents of a teen killed by a drunk driver.)

- If I don't feel like forgiving, it can't be genuine. (Do feelings follow actions, or vice versa?)

- I can't forgive until the other person asks for it. (Thank God he doesn't do that to you.)

- To forgive, I must pretend like nothing happened. (Tell that to Jesus on the cross.)

- I must forgive right away, or it doesn't count. (You're human, not God.)

- Forgiveness always means reconciliation. (Reconciliation takes two; forgiveness takes one.)

Pray that you see through the myths of forgiveness and forgive as you've been forgiven.

❋ SPRING ❋

Build a Life Together

In 1955 Marylin Monroe starred in The Seven Year Itch. *That title has become a cliché for a critical juncture in a marriage—that after seven years in a relationship, happiness starts to fade. Do you believe it?*

Where morning dawns, where evening fades, you call forth songs of joy. PSALM 65:8

The psalmist knew God. He wrote in an earlier verse, "When we were overwhelmed by sins, you forgave our transgressions" (Psalm 65:3). Hope and joy flow from God's forgiveness. Morning, evening, year after year, it doesn't fade. When the purpose of your marriage is singing a song of joy to the Lord, it won't fade either.

In *The Story of Us,* a wife tells how she gave her husband a plastic spoon as a gift for their first anniversary. This spoon was special because they had used it to share their first bowl of wonton soup in the park. Her husband was thrilled to receive it as an anniversary gift. But then, over time, as the couple drifted apart, that spoon began to lose its meaning. "I keep asking myself," she says, "when is that moment in a marriage when a spoon becomes just a spoon?"

It doesn't have to become just a spoon. The specialness doesn't reside in the *spoon;* it resides in *how you look at it.* Your marriage is sacred regardless of how you see it, but how you see your marriage will keep it special and show its sacredness.

Do you know what your spouse wants and loves? Salted cashews? Fresh flowers? Working in the garden? Paris? Golf? Certain sex acts? Saturdays? If your first response is, "I don't know," then how is your spouse supposed to know? So let's start the conversation.

- Ask, "Honey, what do you really like?"

Pray that you never tire of praising God for his grace or keeping your marriage special.

31

❋ SPRING ❋

Build a Life Together

If you could have a time in your marriage back to hold on to it, what would it be? Peter had a moment like that.

Peter said to Jesus, "Lord, it is good for us to be here. If you wish, I will put up three shelters—one for you, one for Moses and one for Elijah." MATTHEW 17:4

Peter was beholding the glory of God and the fulfillment of his promises in those dead but living characters. He didn't want to leave, and you can't blame him. Still, the sight of glory and the voice of the Father encouraged him for the rest of his life, especially in times of doubt.

Not every moment is special. Even though we love Jesus and enjoy his grace, we don't live every moment feeling like we're on the mountain with Peter. Some days are special, and some days you just have to eat your frogs—that is, you just have to do what needs to be done even if it's unpleasant.

You can't always give the extra time, the extra day, or the extra whatever. But when you can, hug longer, give a back rub for 30 minutes instead of 30 seconds, write a card instead of a text, or open a bottle of wine even if it's just with your mac 'n' cheese.

Look closely. It's not the lack of having more that takes the shine off a marriage. If that were the case, the wealthy would never divorce. It's the lack of attention to detail. It's like having kids—if you don't relish them, pay attention to them, and enjoy them when they're growing up, you'll miss so much. Likewise, in marriage, you'll miss much if you don't pay attention to the details of your spouse.

- Write four details you appreciate about your spouse. Then tell each other.

Pray that you pay more attention to your spouse.

Build a Life Together

Traditions might seem like the opposite of special, but not really. Traditions give you something to look forward to and make your family unique.

Every year Jesus' parents went to Jerusalem for the Festival of the Passover. When he was twelve years old, they went up to the festival, according to the custom. LUKE 2:41,42

Customs, traditions, and rituals are part of every culture and every church. Most aren't commanded in Scripture, but they help us do or recall what's important. For example, when we come together for worship, we don't have to include a litany of confession and absolution, nor do we have to pray the Lord's Prayer, but we agree they're good customs. They remind us of what's important and bond us together.

What family traditions bind you together? Likely, some are built around food. You can reconnect at the end of the day. It's a consistent time for devotion and prayer. But it's not the food that makes it special, it's the predictability. You can find great value around any predictable shared time, whether it's routine carpooling, a walk after every dinner, or a weekly date night.

Lovemaking can become predictable too. Some say if things get boring in the bedroom to try some new routines. Maybe, but there's also value in predictability—enjoyable rituals that satisfy you both. Don't feel bad if you like your predictable sex; predictable sex can be the best sex. Scheduled sex is better for both of you than no sex.

Tell each other:

- A current ritual I like is . . .

- Can we explore a tradition like . . .?

Pray that you find meaning in your worship traditions and learn to treasure your family traditions.

Trust

Trust is no accident. It's built up very slowly over time. There are no shortcuts to it. It can be lost quickly, but it is rebuilt much more slowly. What are you doing to build trust?

It is God who makes both us and you stand firm in Christ. He anointed us, set his seal of ownership on us, and put his Spirit in our hearts as a deposit, guaranteeing what is to come. 2 CORINTHIANS 1:21,22

God did things in the past that guarantee other things in the future. In the Sacrament of Baptism, he anointed you, set his seal on you, and put his Spirit into your heart. His past actions guarantee your future.

Your trust in each other is based on things you've done in the past. You've promised God that you'll live together as husband and wife. You've promised each other that you'll treat each other as Jesus treats you, his church. Those promises guarantee your future.

How are you doing with those promises? As you keep them, you build trust. Marriage is made up of hundreds of things you say and do that either build your trust or chip away at it. Focus on building it.

- Recall promises God has made to you and kept for you. Don't rush. Take a few minutes and reflect personally. Then compare your recollections of God's promises.

- Tell your spouse one thing he or she does that leads you to trust his or her promises.

Pray that you hear God's promises when you worship in church this week and thank him for his faithfulness. Pray that you build on the actions you talked about that build trust in your marriage.

❋ SPRING ❋

Trust

❖

The opening scene in the movie Sliding Doors *plays twice. In one, the main character misses a train. In the other, she catches a train. The rest of the movie shows two ways her life would have gone from the two opening scenes. Have you ever thought about how one seemingly small thing made a big difference in your life or marriage?*

God will credit righteousness—for us who believe in him who raised Jesus our Lord from the dead. ROMANS 4:24

Your baptism into Christ and the faith that came with it was just one apparently little thing, but everything in your life is different because of it. Through it, you have credit for Jesus' sinless life. Jesus' empty grave proves it. Turns out your baptism was no little thing.

Because you build trust through hundreds of *little things* you say to and do for each other, it's easy to miss how important they are. Those little things do more to build trust than one big thing, like perhaps a surprise trip to Paris. Although you might argue for the vacation!

- Individually write a script of five ways your life is better because you're married to your spouse. Get creative:

  1.

  2.

  3.

  4.

  5.

Pray with thanksgiving for God's gift of Jesus' righteousness, and ask him to help you remember that the small things in your marriage aren't small at all.

❁ SPRING ❁

Trust

The physical clothes you're wearing aren't the only ones you put on today. Wear these spiritual clothes to build trust:

As God's chosen people, holy and dearly loved, clothe yourselves with compassion, kindness, humility, gentleness and patience. COLOSSIANS 3:12

"Clothe yourselves with compassion." It means to feel with someone or walk in someone else's shoes. But more than just feeling for someone, compassion wants to do something about it.

Jesus is God with a human body; he knows what it's like to walk about on earth. Jesus is true man, so he could demonstrate the human characteristic of compassion. Think of an event in Jesus' life when he demonstrated compassion. If you would rather research this on your own, don't read further! But here's one example: Jesus met a young man confused about God's moral law and loved him (Mark 10:21). He put himself in the man's shoes and knew how easy it would be to imagine that our goodness is good enough for God. But Jesus' compassion moved him to do more than just feel sorry for the man. Jesus did something. He proceeded to live a sinless life to give the goodness the man needed. Jesus' compassion moves him to provide us with the goodness we need too: his goodness.

Jesus' compassion moves us to trust him. Likewise, your compassion for your spouse moves him or her to trust you. What would compassion look like in your marriage?

- Complete the following sentence privately, and then read your sentence to your spouse. "I really felt you knew what I needed and acted to help me when you . . ."

- Tell each other how you felt that time when he or she showed you compassion.

Pray that you learn how to put on compassion from Jesus and from your spouse.

❄ SPRING ❄

Pursue Friendship

When God created the world, he declared what he had made "good" six times. After God created the first man, though, he declared something else.

The LORD God said, "It is not good for the man to be alone. I will make a helper suitable for him." GENESIS 2:18

The three persons of the triune God enjoy a perfect relationship, but man alone wouldn't have that blessing with another human. A dog is nice, but . . .

So the Lord created a "helper" for him. The Hebrew word is *ayzer* and can mean a "helper," "companion," "complement," or "friend." Don't see anything inferior in the word "helper." God calls himself by that same name six times in the Psalms. At last check, he is not inferior to us.

How do you define *friendship*? Common definitions include words like *faithful, loyal,* and *sympathetic.* You don't have to walk on eggshells around a friend because you're comfortable and trust you'll take each other's words in the best way.

Friendship is what happens when you have common interests and longings for the same thing. Erotic love is two people looking at each other and being moved; friendship is two people looking at the same thing and being stirred by it together. Unfortunately, social media has watered down the meaning of *friend.* What are you doing to infuse richness into your friendship?

- Individually write a definition of *friendship.* When you're done, read it to your spouse and ask, "What can I do to pursue that with you?"

Pray that you value God's gift of *friendship* with your spouse and pursue it passionately.

Pursue Friendship

We enjoy different kinds of friendships. Make yours a spiritual friendship.

Dear friends, now we are children of God, and what we will be has not yet been made known. But we know that when Christ appears, we shall be like him, for we shall see him as he is. 1 JOHN 3:2

Natural friendships develop among those who read the same author or find themselves in the same stage of parenting. Spiritual friendship happens when you share a passion for helping each other to a common destination: standing face-to-face with Jesus "when [he] appears." The horizon seems far away, but we pursue it confidently because we are God's children.

We each have an old self and a new self. The old self is crippled with anxieties, bad habits, and character flaws. The new self is freed from sin and flaws, but it's also a work in progress. Living together gives you a glimpse of the person God is shaping. It's exciting to see what God is doing in you and in your spouse. Together you'll stand before Jesus perfect and pure and exclaim, "I knew it!"

Jesus made the creation of our new selves his priority to the point of his death on a cross. Only as we love Jesus first will we imitate him by putting our spouse first. When we do, we're pursuing spiritual friendship.

We can learn from others. You can't force friendship with other couples at church, but you can stay near them and see what develops. Small groups in a church can be helpful for that.

- Individually write a definition of *spiritual* friendship. Read it to your spouse and discuss, "What can we do to pursue that together?"

Pray that you keep the end in mind: standing face-to-face with Jesus.

❊ SPRING ❊

Pursue Friendship

Paul used physical health to describe both the church and marriage.

Husbands ought to love their wives as their own bodies. He who loves his wife loves himself. After all, no one ever hated their own body, but they feed and care for their body, just as Christ does the church. EPHESIANS 5:28,29

God made marriage foundational, like the health of your body. Make marriage a sidebar to your career, hobby, or children, and you weaken it. If your marriage is weak, other success in life won't matter as much. If your marriage is healthy, even other difficulties won't matter as much. God gave marriage the power to set the course for your whole life. Your friendship with your spouse deserves to be your priority. When something else consumes more attention than your spouse, it can destroy a marriage.

Yes, children need you. Parenting is a high calling God gives some. But if you put your child's music, sports, etc., ahead of your marriage, it will hurt the child and may kill the marriage. God put a husband and a wife in the Garden of Eden, not a parent and a child.

Yes, your work matters to God, not to mention the bank that holds your mortgage. But if someone or something else gets all your creativity, energy, and time, your spouse may rightly conclude you're not putting him or her first. Your friendship will suffer.

See your spouse as not just your lover, financial partner, or co-parent but as your best and spiritual friend. Then your marriage will be your most fulfilling and important human relationship.

Finish each sentence.

- You might be overcommitted to your career if . . .

- You might be overcommitted to your children if . . .

- You might be overcommitted to your parents if . . .

Pray that you make friendship with each other a priority.

Communicate With Each Other

Assertiveness is an important communication skill. It's important to state what you want and how you feel.

God can testify how I long for all of you with the affection of Christ Jesus. PHILIPPIANS 1:8

Throughout the gospels, Jesus feels. He is described as compassionate, angry, troubled, grieved, glad, and sad. Jesus, fully human, expressed how he felt and what he wanted. But Jesus is God. His emotions didn't control him; they only showed him to be human. When he communicated with people, he was assertive. He clearly stated what he wanted and how he felt.

It's no surprise that Jesus was a master communicator. It is surprising how hard it is to be assertive without being selfish or insensitive. You may have been taught from childhood not to use the *I* word. You were taught well. Too many *I* sentences can become tiresome. But too few *I* sentences, especially about what you want and how you feel, leave both you and your spouse frustrated. You haven't communicated your feelings clearly, and your spouse has missed out on knowing what is on your heart.

Try it this week. Force yourself to say, "I feel . . ." and continue with one of the four emotions: mad, glad, sad, or scared. Don't say it to place blame; say it to communicate your feelings. Resist shifting into blame mode by continuing, "I feel that you . . ." No, this is about *your* feelings.

- Determine differences between these sentences: "You were so inconsiderate of me in front of your friends," and "I felt hurt when you ignored me in front of your friends."

- Tell each other reasons you find assertiveness difficult (or easy!).

Pray that you better appreciate Jesus' emotions as you read the gospels and that you could be assertive without blaming or becoming selfish.

Communicate With Each Other

Body language communicates. Talking with someone while looking that person in the eye displays a high level of engagement. Speaking at someone while walking away reveals just the opposite.

**Jesus turned and saw her. "Take heart, daughter,"
he said, "your faith has healed you."** MATTHEW 9:22

Jesus didn't have to stop, turn, and look at her. He could have kept walking, thrown a wave at her, and talked over his shoulder. She would have been healed just as wholly, but she wouldn't have known Jesus' heart. And Jesus wanted her to know his heart and the value of the faith he'd given her.

Husbands and wives do dishes shoulder to shoulder, ride in the car shoulder to shoulder, cheer on their child's sports team shoulder to shoulder, and probably watch television shoulder to shoulder.

Your marriage will benefit from getting eye to eye. Turn your chairs so you're not shoulder to shoulder facing the television but toe to toe facing each other. Your body language will communicate, "You matter more to me than anything else in this room." Give it a try. The television will survive without you. You might even permanently arrange your furniture around what or who is most important in the room.

- Try it with this devotion or, if it's too late, the next one. Arrange your chairs so you're toe to toe, knee to knee, and hand in hand as you read, pray, and do the activity.

- Use a concordance, Bible app, or an internet search to find events when "Jesus turned." Determine what you learn about Jesus from each.

Pray that you appreciate Jesus turning toward you, distraction-free, and pray that you could have the wisdom and awareness to turn toward each other.

 **☀ SUMMER ☀**

Communicate With Each Other

Have you noticed a husband and a wife at a restaurant staring at their phones? Or acting like the painting on the wall is more interesting than their mate? How do you know they're married? Because dating people don't do that.

Enjoy life with your wife, whom you love, all the days of this meaningless life that God has given you under the sun. ECCLESIASTES 9:9

Even though the best moments of our lives are fleeting, they are gifts from God. Wise Solomon gives you permission to enjoy them. Consider your marriage a gift of God to be enjoyed in his earthly kingdom. You'll enjoy each other too in his heavenly kingdom—just in a different, better way. Engage with each other like the gifts from God that you are.

Here are three ideas to spark your conversation. Try them out. When you go out on your next date night, fool the people around you into thinking you're a newly dating couple as you enjoy (re)connecting with your spouse.

- **Five-question habit:** You're not allowed to stop the conversation or change the subject until you ask five questions on the topic your spouse just brought up. Don't give up. Sometimes the fifth question is the most important.

- **Take an interest:** Your spouse's thing may not be your thing at all, but you can take an interest. Read a book, watch a video, or even take a class on it—not to compete but to know your spouse and be able to talk about his or her thing.

- **Forget about formulating your response:** Instead of thinking, *What am I going to say next?* train yourself to think, *What is she or he going to say next?* See how good you can get at guessing.

Pray that you receive God's earthly gifts with thanksgiving, including conversation with each other.

☀ SUMMER ☀

Appreciate Each Other

What kind of art do you appreciate? Modern sculpture? Ballet? Country music? A sunset? Highbrow or down-home, we all have some type of art we appreciate. Would it surprise you to hear that God calls you his artwork?

We are God's handiwork, created in Christ Jesus to do good works, which God prepared in advance for us to do. EPHESIANS 2:10

The word *handiwork* is the Greek word *poiēma,* from which we get our word *poem.* You are God's artwork. He created you "in Christ Jesus," which Paul usually refers to as the new self. You weren't born a child of God; the Spirit made you a child of God. He also crafted you with certain gifts, abilities, experiences, strengths, and even weaknesses. That means, of course, your spouse is also a work of art.

- Circle three words you think describe your spouse.

Sensitive	Considerate	Calm
Brave	Organized	Practical
Intelligent	Cheerful	Humble
Energetic	Gracious	Gentle
Decisive	Caring	Reliable
Fun	Self-controlled	Witty
Sexy	Thrifty	Protective
Patient	Adventurous	Industrious

- Tell your spouse one story about each word you circled to illustrate that characteristic.

Pray that you look for these characteristics in your spouse, thank God for the blessings they bring to your marriage, and tell your spouse how much you appreciate them in him or her.

Appreciate Each Other

❖

Why are you reading this devotion? What goals do you have in working through these studies with your spouse?

[Jesus said,] "I am the vine; you are the branches. If you remain in me and I in you, you will bear much fruit." JOHN 15:5

The first reason to work through these meditations on God's Word isn't to make your marriage better. It isn't to be a better husband, father, mother, or wife. It's to stay connected to Jesus. Satan, our sinful flesh, and the world want to take us away from Jesus. The result of that wouldn't just be a lousy family—it would be losing the eternal life Jesus won for us.

We pick up God's Word with the prayer and confidence of staying connected to Jesus. Out of that relationship to Jesus comes the functions of being a better husband, father, wife, or mother, as well as a better employee, citizen, friend, and more.

Some fruit lasts longer than others; peaches don't seem to last as long as apples. Some "fruit" we bear will last for eternity: baptizing our children, supporting gospel preaching and teaching, feeding our own faith. Some fruit we bear will be shorter-lived. I don't know if doing one of your spouse's normal chores will be etched in the halls of glory or if filling up your spouse's gas tank will make the angels sing an anthem. But God won't forget; he sees it as the fruit we bear to show our thanksgiving to him. Jesus first, fruit second.

- Review what you do together to stay connected to Jesus. How do you use his Word and sacrament?

- Tell your spouse one fruit of faith you are seeing in him or her these days.

Pray that you see the value of staying connected to Jesus and bearing much fruit in your marriage.

Appreciate Each Other

In your marriage, you're either moving toward enhancing the glory of your spouse or degrading your spouse. To understand that, we have to understand glory.

> **"Holy, holy, holy is the Lord Almighty;
> the whole earth is full of his glory."** ISAIAH 6:3
>
> **[Jesus said,] "I have given them the glory
> that you gave me."** JOHN 17:22

Isaiah heard angels singing about the Lord's glory. Jesus prayed about giving you glory. We must be talking about two different kinds of glory.

God's glory originates with him. It is his goodness, mercy, and compassion. His glory fills the earth. We can't add to it, but we can acknowledge it by trusting him, praising him, and thanking him. We call that giving God glory.

The glory Jesus speaks of giving us is reflected, not original. We reflect God's glory when we treat each other as an equal recipient of his glory. You might even call that the purpose of marriage: to give God glory and enhance the glory of your spouse.

The order is critical. First, give glory to God by believing his Word and promise. Second, give your spouse a different kind of glory—the kind that comes from giving your spouse importance, influence, and appreciation.

- Complete the following sentences individually. Then tell your spouse what you wrote.

  One reason I'm grateful for your influence on me is . . .

  One way you've influenced our marriage is . . .

  I think I should give you more importance when it comes to . . .

Pray that you seek to glorify Jesus by giving him more importance and influence in your life and enhance your spouse's glory by giving him or her importance and influence in your decisions.

Manage Conflict

Walt Disney said, "If you can dream it, you can do it" (although there's some debate about whether he was the first to say it). What difference could it make in your marriage if you focused on the present and dreamed about the future rather than dwelling on the past?

"In your anger do not sin": Do not let the sun go down while you are still angry, and do not give the devil a foothold. EPHESIANS 4:26,27

You've probably heard Paul's words above as marriage advice. In Ephesians 5:1,2, Paul highlighted Christ's love for the world. In Ephesians 5:22-28, Paul highlighted Christ's love for you and your spouse. In our verses here, Paul highlighted your need to understand your spouse. Neglect your focus on Christ's love for the world, and it will take you out of your mission and maybe lead to bigotry. Neglect your focus on Christ's love for you and your spouse, and it will harm your faith. Neglect the discipline of seeking to understand your spouse, and it will hurt your relationship. Do this the next time you're in church:

- Record specific Bible verses you heard in the service that focused your attention on 1-3 below. Record them privately and discuss them after church.

  1. Christ's love for the world:

  2. Christ's love for you:

  3. Christ's love for your spouse:

Pray that the Word of God helps you focus on Christ's love for you and helps you understand your spouse.

Manage Conflict

When there's a conflict at work, are you more likely to ignore it and hope it goes away or face it and fight it? What about in your marriage?

All have sinned and fall short of the glory of God, and all are justified freely by his grace through the redemption that came by Christ Jesus. ROMANS 3:23,24

We all have a conflict with God. It's called sin. But God acted to resolve it; the cost was infinite, but the result is eternal. You are justified and redeemed. God has removed your conflict with him.

However, husbands and wives *cannot* not have conflict with each other. It's how we respond to it that makes all the difference. Couples in happy marriages are better able to move through conflict because they're more likely to (1) feel understood, (2) resolve differences with a plan, and (3) take the disagreements seriously. It makes sense. The question is, How will we pursue these things?

On the other hand, other actions seem to only make things worse. Like these:

1. One spouse ends up feeling responsible for the problem.

2. One spouse goes out of the way to avoid conflict with the other.

3. We have different ideas of the best way to solve disagreements.

4. Some of our differences never seem to get resolved.

5. We sometimes have serious disputes over unimportant things.

Turn to your spouse and ask, "Which one of these might be an issue in the way we handle conflict in our marriage?" It's time to listen and learn, not to get defensive or panic.

Pray that you thank God daily for how he has settled your conflict with him, and ask him to show you actions to help you move through conflict with your spouse.

Manage Conflict

President Barack Obama said, "You can't always come up with the optimal solution, but you can usually come up with a better solution. A good compromise, a good piece of legislation, is like a good sentence." How well do the two of you compose that sentence?*

Submit to one another out of reverence for Christ. EPHESIANS 5:21

Who wants to submit? It sounds degrading and abusive until you read the gospel. Jesus submitted to his Father, but he wasn't inferior to him, nor did the Father abuse him. Jesus chose to put his Father's will ahead of his own out of love for his Father and love for you. Because he loved you to the point of dying as the payment for sin, you can sleep well tonight. You've received grace.

Compromise is one way you can manage conflict and submit to your spouse out of reverence for Christ.

Clarify one conflict. Start small: where to vacation, fix the car or get another, etc. Each of you draw a circle about 5 inches in diameter. Inside that circle, draw another circle about 1 inch in diameter. Then write in the smaller circle one or two things you feel you can't compromise on. In the larger circle, write all the things you're flexible on, as many as you can.

Agree on a time to exchange diagrams. Ask each other:

- What do we agree on?

- What are our common goals and feelings?

- Why are your inflexible items so important to you?

- Can we find a temporary compromise?

- Pray, "How can I put my spouse first in this?"

Pray that you appreciate all the more how Jesus put you ahead of himself, and ask him to help you put your spouse ahead of yourself.

---

*https://www.newyorker.com/magazine/2004/05/31/the-candidate-5

Serve Each Other

Find three lessons Jesus taught about serving in these verses:

[Jesus] got up from the meal, took off his outer clothing, and wrapped a towel around his waist. After that, he poured water into a basin and began to wash his disciples' feet, drying them with the towel that was wrapped around him. He came to Simon Peter, who said to him, "Lord, are you going to wash my feet?" When he had finished washing their feet, he put on his clothes and returned to his place. "Do you understand what I have done for you?" he asked them. "Now that I, your Lord and Teacher, have washed your feet, you also should wash one another's feet." JOHN 13:4-6,12,14

Which three did you find? Let's compare.

One: Serving meets a genuine need. The disciples' feet were dirty, and they reclined close to each other. Enough said. If you can't find practical ways to serve your spouse, you're not really looking.

Two: At least one person felt uncomfortable being served. Do you not communicate your needs because you don't want to be a bother? Admirable as that may be, you also then leave your spouse guessing about how to serve you.

Three: Even the greatest is to be a servant. No one in the room was greater than Jesus. No one in the world was greater than Jesus. But when it came to serving, he went first.

- Determine to serve your spouse tomorrow in one expected practical way.

- Ask each other, "Is there something you'd like me to do that you hesitate to ask for?"

- Notice your spouse serving you and compliment him or her for such "greatness."

Pray that you appreciate Jesus' humility in serving you. Ask for his help in serving each other.

☀ SUMMER ☀

Serve Each Other

Why we serve one another matters. You do your job to get a paycheck. You serve your spouse for other reasons.

Love must be sincere. Hate what is evil; cling to what is good. Be devoted to one another in love. Honor one another above yourselves. ROMANS 12:9,10

No one ever lived out the qualities of love, sincerity, goodness, devotion, and honor better than the Son of God. The chief purpose of the Bible is to give us such knowledge of him, a growing faith in him, and love for him. The Bible isn't a how-to manual, but it is an "I-want-to" manual. Do you want to respond to God's goodness to you? Then "honor one another above yourselves."

It sounds so chivalrous, maybe even mysterious. But the only honor that does any good is the honor your spouse can see. Here are some avenues to honor. Which ones would make you feel honored? Tell each other an example.

- Ask how you can help, or simply dive in and help without being asked (e.g., cleaning the shower).

- Never remind your spouse of past mistakes, especially in front of others.

- Remember special dates. They may not mean much to you but might mean the world to your spouse. And it's not all about you.

- Eat meals together with no screens at the table. Your spouse is always more worthy of honor than something online.

- Talk over decisions with your spouse *before* they are made—even the minor ones.

- Compliment your spouse's progress in something (e.g., listening, being more sensitive, etc.).

Pray that you are so moved by the ways Jesus has honored you that you look for ways to honor your spouse.

Serve Each Other

❖

Would you serve peanut butter sandwiches after a Thanksgiving Day meal? Of course not; no one needs it. How well do you know what your spouse needs?

[Jesus said,] "Even the Son of Man did not come to be served, but to serve, and to give his life as a ransom for many." MARK 10:45

Jesus didn't need to discover what I needed. He's God. He knew I needed his righteousness. He gave me exactly what I needed.

Christians spouses say, "I want to serve you because Jesus has served me. I want to learn what your needs are so I can meet them."

If I think treating my spouse the way I like to be treated will meet his or her needs, I'll seldom get it right. Anyone who has been married more than, say, ten minutes knows you're not the same. Your spouse is your best coach in helping you meet his or her needs.

Mark the five items in the list below you think you need most from your spouse, and mark in a different way the five items you think *your spouse* will say he or she needs most from you. Set a date night to compare your lists. You may ask questions, but you may not disagree.

- o Admiration
- o Career support
- o Companionship and friendship
- o Domestic support
- o Emotional intimacy
- o Communication
- o Encouragement and affirmation
- o Family relationships
- o Honesty and openness
- o Nonsexual touch
- o Personal time
- o Romance
- o Security and stability
- o Sexual intimacy
- o Significance
- o Spiritual intimacy
- o To be desired
- o To provide and protect
- o Trust
- o Unconditional love and acceptance
- o Understanding and empathy

Pray that you discover your spouse's needs and ask for help in meeting them.

☀ SUMMER ☀

Spiritual Intimacy

You have opportunities to nurture your spiritual life together that you didn't have when you were single. Give thanks for that, and remember to pray for your single friends.

**Glorify the LORD with me;
let us exalt his name together.** PSALM 34:3

The glory of God is everything God is and how he chooses to reveal it. The greatest glory of God is his grace, and we glorify him by believing it and living according to his Word.

The gospel is what makes Christianity different from every other religion. All religions have some kind of morality. In fact, ancient Norse, Greek, and Eastern religions have codes of morality similar to the Ten Commandments. Even the atheist says he lives by some kind of Golden Rule. But he doesn't. And Christians don't either. No one except Christ has lived like that. Jesus doesn't promise to show us God or put us on the path to God. He *is* God who came to us. Where we and all humanity fell short, Jesus didn't. He lived for sinners. He died for sinners. He rose from the dead to show us what's in store for all who trust in him. Do you see why trusting in him is the greatest way we glorify him?

However, there's more to glorifying God. When you love your wife, you're glorifying God. When you respect your husband, you're glorifying God. When you ensure that you both hear God's Word and receive the sacrament, you're glorifying God.

- Work together to create a list of ten things you do in your marriage to glorify God and respond to his grace.

Pray that your single friends find encouragement to glorify God with you and that you find ways to glorify him together.

Spiritual Intimacy

Read the following verses and describe how this was true or not true in your home growing up.

> **"Now fear the LORD and serve him with all faithfulness. Throw away the gods your ancestors worshiped beyond the Euphrates River and in Egypt, and serve the LORD. But if serving the LORD seems undesirable to you, then choose for yourselves this day whom you will serve, whether the gods your ancestors served beyond the Euphrates, or the gods of the Amorites, in whose land you are living. But as for me and my household, we will serve the LORD."** JOSHUA 24:14,15

If this was true in your home growing up, you probably spoke about regular church attendance, Sunday school, and parents who monitored what you watched and where you went. They encouraged you to have godly friends and make God-pleasing choices. If this wasn't true in your home growing up, you probably recalled having more freedoms than were good for you, few if any memories of church, and little if any Bible teaching. This isn't to say your parents didn't love you; they just didn't love you with a desire to serve the Lord.

And now you're reading a Christian book on marriage. What happened? God happened.

Isn't it great that God gives us two families, one by birth and one by new birth? That you're seeking to become more spiritually intimate with your spouse means you're doing great. You say with Joshua, "We will serve the Lord." Thank God.

- Name some gods of our culture that you have thrown away.

Joshua's example blessed the people of Israel. Pray for others to be blessed by your example to serve the Lord.

Pray that you serve the Lord and have the courage to reject the false gods of our times.

Spiritual Intimacy

When two objects get closer to a third object, the first two objects are also closer to each other. The closer you both draw to God, the closer you'll be to each other.

Let us draw near to God with a sincere heart and with the full assurance that faith brings, having our hearts sprinkled to cleanse us from a guilty conscience and having our bodies washed with pure water. HEBREWS 10:22

The writer to the Hebrews called us out on our real problem: the need for cleansing every resource in our life. We use our resources to sin, but Jesus used all his resources to cleanse us from sin. You can tell your conscience, "You can't condemn me because Jesus was condemned for me." You can recall your baptism and know you're pure in God's eyes. Then you can look at your spouse and say, "He's the one we need. Let's draw near to him together."

The 17th-century French mathematician Blaise Pascal wrote, "There is a God-shaped vacuum in the heart of every man which cannot be satisfied by any created thing but only by God, the Creator, who is made known through Jesus Christ." Christian liturgies have acknowledged that and invited worshipers, "Let us draw near with a true heart and confess our sins." We do so with the full assurance of his response: forgiveness.

Confess your sins together. You will grow spiritually intimate.

- Discuss the time of confession and absolution (announcement of forgiveness) in your church. What do you find most helpful? How do you make it more personal?

Pray that your confession and absolution in church draw you closer together.

Get On the Same Page With Your Finances

Should a Christian tithe from gross income (the big number) or from net (the take-home pay)?

Be sure to set aside a tenth of all that your fields produce each year. DEUTERONOMY 14:22

That settles it, right? Yes, we learn something about giving from the Old Testament. This ten percent, the tithe, was only one form of giving required. Other required offerings added up to about a third of a family's annual income.

But now, we aren't under the commands of the Old Testament. Jesus obeyed them for us and set us free. If he hadn't, you couldn't have enjoyed that bacon (another reason to praise him). And your church could levy a tax on you.

Paul knew the command to tithe better than most. Yet he wrote, "You will be enriched in every way so that you can be generous on every occasion, and through us your generosity will result in thanksgiving to God" (2 Corinthians 9:11). Generosity is the guiding principle for New Testament believers. The Bible also teaches us to give proportionately, regularly, and first.

If something about that opening question bothered you, good. You don't have to answer every question. The first word was a red flag: *should. Should?* Generosity doesn't ask *should.* Generosity looks for ways to give more because it wants to. And often, a tithe is just a starting point.

If your church hasn't taught this in a while, gently ask your pastor to do so. We all need it.

- Write the steps you use in determining how, when, and how much you will give in the next year.

- Discuss what you'd like to change on your list.

Pray that you find joy in giving generously, as you have generously received.

Get On the Same Page With Your Finances

Most couples see eye to eye on some things but not on everything. Where are your views of money similar, and where are they different?

**"Give back to Caesar what is Caesar's,
and to God what is God's."** LUKE 20:25

Jesus didn't talk much about money. He did express dismay at how often people wanted to talk about it. Sit in a few church meetings and you see the same thing. Not many have much to say about the evangelism plan, but bring up the budget and count on input. Plenty of input. That's not all bad. Money is another gift of God to be used for his purposes, but how we see it goes deeper. How do you see it?

Do you tend to view money as:

1. capable of making you look good? (new clothes, status car, bigger mortgage, etc.)

2. security? (striving to build your 401(k), five-figure emergency fund, going without now to have more for later, etc.)

3. a means to enjoyment? (vacations, entertaining others, sports, etc.)

4. a way of controlling your life? (pay someone else to do unpleasant chores, retirement goals, fly instead of drive, etc.)

Those aren't wrong views of money—just views. You don't have to see it the same way, but it helps to know how you each view your money.

- Review the four views of money. Privately rank them in the order you feel you view money, and then tell each other. The goal isn't to solve anything but just to understand each other better.

Pray that you accept each other, even your different views of money.

Get On the Same Page With Your Finances

Why do people argue about money? Most reasons have little to do with how much they have.

What causes fights and quarrels among you? Don't they come from your desires that battle within you? JAMES 4:1

We are, at the core, self-centered and proud. We want to use our limited time, energy, and money the way we want to. But to do so pushes away our spouse and even God. Jesus' desire was more for you than for himself. That's why he stayed on the cross. When he came out of his grave, he demonstrated just how rich you are. You have the same resurrection coming. So what's left to fight about?

Okay, so let's be real: money. Here are four reasons couples tend to argue about money.

1. Tension over family. If there's chaos and disorder in how we make family decisions and we lack a clear guide for spending money, we'll never be done arguing about priorities.

2. Conflict over who gets to spend how much on what. No couple has unlimited means, so if you spend it, I can't. I may not like that.

3. One tends to be a diligent spender and the other a diligent saver. This may just be the greatest evidence of the Lord's sense of humor: He gave you to each other.

4. Different views of what money can and can't do. You'd think we'd learn that money can't buy happiness, but we don't.

Do any of those feel familiar? If not, give thanks. If so, try this:

- Determine how Jesus' resurrection and his promise of your resurrection can change it.

Pray that you see the solution to your arguments over money in the gospel.

Know Each Other

To be intimate with someone is to know what others don't know about him or her. Husbands, when you find yourself browsing for a gift for your wife in the intimate apparel section of the department store, you're just being biblical, right? Perhaps that's a stretch, but read this:

> **Adam knew Eve his wife; and she conceived, and bare Cain.** GENESIS 4:1 (KJV)

The biblical word for a husband and wife making love is the Hebrew word *yadah*—"to know." Couples who aren't having sex regularly other than for obvious physical or distance reasons are missing God's plan for knowing each other. If that's you, get some help and work through the emotional or conflict issues. Get back to knowing each other.

The Spirit used the same word, *yadah,* to describe our relationship with God in the new covenant of his grace. We heard it a few devotions earlier: " 'They will all know me, from the least of them to the greatest,' declares the LORD. 'For I will forgive their wickedness and will remember their sins no more' " (Jeremiah 31:34). God has determined to know you by his grace.

Knowing each other isn't the same as knowing God. But when you know each other, you get a little picture of what it is to know God. No wonder we long to *know* each other sexually, and we long to know God by his grace.

Commit right now to doing at least one of the following:

- Find your spouse's favorite book and read it.

- Find your spouse's favorite play and get tickets to it.

- Find out what language your spouse has always dreamed of learning and get an easy online introduction course.

Pray that you will continue to learn about each other, and in that knowledge, continue to know God's gift of sex too.

Know Each Other

Have you found it challenging to give your full attention to your spouse but easy to give your attention to the beep of a new text or social media post? Psychology offers some interesting reasons why, but the Lord who invented psychology has a thing or two to say about giving attention.

Moses and Aaron, Nadab and Abihu, and the seventy elders of Israel went up and saw the God of Israel. . . . But God did not raise his hand against these leaders of the Israelites; they saw God, and they ate and drank. EXODUS 24:9-11

The same God who invited these people to lunch later told Moses, "No one may see me and live" (Exodus 33:20). How can both be true? God's nature is how. God hates sin so sinners can't stand in his presence. God has compassion on the sinner. That was made clear when he sent his Son to live and die in the sinner's place. In Jesus, God turns his face toward us.

He pays attention to you and your spouse better than you ever will. He doesn't overlook your sin; he pays for it. And he has compassion on you both.

Husbands and wives aren't called to overlook the other's sin, but neither are they called to fix it. That's God's job. Let him do it. Give your attention to the best of your spouse. God did that and invited sinners to lunch. Time for a lunch date?

- The next time you're dining out, look for couples who aren't paying attention to each other. Pray for them.

- Agree to put your phones in a basket or another room during meals.

Pray that you thank God for his attention to you and that he looks on you and your spouse with grace.

Know Each Other

"Oh, I just assumed . . ." Has that ever gotten you into trouble? A prophet who lived six hundred years before Jesus was born assumed some things about God. The Lord told him he was preparing the Babylonians to bring his judgment on Israel. Habakkuk complained, "There's no way you would do that." He assumed he knew better than God and concluded:

I will stand at my watch and station myself on the ramparts; I will look to see what he will say to me, and what answer I am to give to this complaint. HABAKKUK 2:1

The Lord's answer was not what Habakkuk assumed it would be. The Lord would follow through and bring his judgment on Israel. But after his people turned back to him, the Lord promised to bring woe on Babylon.

We're prone to assume too much about God and his ways, and he never changes. Imagine how much more likely we are to assume too much about our spouse who is constantly changing! Dreams change. Hopes change. Fears change. Those are the big things. Small things change too, like which car you'd like, which author you prefer, or which beverage you crave. So don't assume too much. Your spouse, unlike your God, is constantly changing.

- Tell each other something you once considered a dream but now don't. You might need to think for a while before you tell each other.

- Take turns completing this sentence: "Three things it's safe for me to assume about you are . . ."

Pray that you give thanks for God's steady character and that you stay in tune to the changes in your spouse.

☀ SUMMER ☀

Connect With Each Other

If you want to better understand your connection with each other, it can be helpful to understand the nature of disconnection.

The wages of sin is death. ROMANS 6:23

Someone who is disconnected from the physical blessings of God is physically dead. Someone who is disconnected from the spiritual blessings of God is spiritually dead, an unbeliever. Someone who is disconnected from the eternal blessings of God is eternally dead. The second kind of death can change; the last kind never does. Hell is disconnection from God. Living hell is disconnection from God's spiritual blessings, which can happen even while a person is physically alive.

Have you heard people call their marriage a living hell? They're disconnected from the one they most want to be connected to—their spouse. It usually settles in slowly, but there are hints that a disconnect is coming. Let their dialogue be a witnessing opportunity for you to point them back to their connection with God through repentance and faith. But let their dialogue also be a warning for you.

- Read this dialogue:
  Tony: I'm hurt because all we ever do anymore is argue.
  Sue: Anymore? As if it used to be different?
  Tony: Yes, it did. And you know it did.
  Sue: Yes, it was different. You have no idea how sad that makes me.
  Tony: So what do you want to do?
  Sue: I have my work, my friends, and my kids.
  Tony: Our kids.
  Sue: Technically, yes.
  Tony: What do you mean by that?
  Sue: What do you think I mean? Who is the real parent here?
  Tony: That is unfair. I have to work. What would we do if I didn't bring in the money?
  Sue: That's your excuse.
  Tony: I can't believe how cruel you've become.
  Sue: I can't believe how clueless you've become.

Describe Tony's feelings. Describe Sue's feelings.

Pray that you appreciate your physical, spiritual, and eternal blessings, and that you see warning signs of a disconnect with each other.

Connect With Each Other

Radon is an odorless, colorless gas that seeps into homes through cracks in the foundation and has become a leading cause of lung cancer. Distraction is like that in marriage. It often seeps in undetected, divides your attention, and prevents concentration.

"Martha, Martha," the Lord answered, "you are worried and upset about many things, but few things are needed— or indeed only one. Mary has chosen what is better, and it will not be taken away from her." LUKE 10:41,42

It is easy to identify bad things as distractions. It is more challenging to identify when good things (like getting a meal ready) have become distractions. Jesus taught the sisters how easy it is to be distracted from important things, even the one crucial thing.

Distraction in marriage is everywhere but hard to see. To detect radon, you put a radon detector in your basement. But how do you detect distractions in your marriage? One way is when talking with other couples—listen for what's distracting them from each other. Pay attention to "time suckers" and "time savers." Identify sources of distraction that can keep you from giving each other the time and attention you need to stay connected.

Intimacy requires uninterrupted time, undivided attention, and a commitment to forego distractions. Discuss which of the following actions might help you detect distractions:

- Turn it off. Rarely has one invention been as useful as the power button on the phone, tablet, television, etc.

- Schedule sex. Sounds unromantic? It's more romantic than no sex or tired sex.

- Spend time with God's Word. Find a way to be in the Word together. It's never a distraction.

- Have a date night. You might be amazed at what one night a week can do to keep you connected.

Pray that you recognize distractions from God and each other.

Connect With Each Other

Kudzu is a fast-growing plant imported to the United States in 1908 to help control erosion. By 1928, the DNR issued a warning that it "could become a pest." Those who live in Georgia know it's a pest. It's possible to have too much of a good thing. Good things might keep us from doing the good works God has planned for us.

For we are God's handiwork, created in Christ Jesus to do good works, which God prepared in advance for us to do. EPHESIANS 2:10

Your Savior has done the good work of living and dying for you. That's grace. Another form of grace is that God has planned good work for you to do.

Information, people, and ideas are more available to us than ever before, but you can have too much of a good thing. If you don't learn to say no to some things, they will become like kudzu and choke out the work God has planned for you.

Don't assume others will set boundaries for you. They won't. What's your strategy for saying no to good work that isn't the good work God has prepared for you to do? Discuss these solutions.

- What works for you as a good off switch to help you shut down and not take on more?

- How can you encourage each other to ask, "Is this the good work God has prepared for me?"

- How difficult is it for you to say no or, "Let me check with my spouse, and I'll get back to you"? If your default answer is yes, you might never get to the good work God has prepared for you.

Pray that you'll understand the good work God has prepared for you to do and that you honor each other as you pursue it.

☀ SUMMER ☀

Enjoy Sexual Intimacy

Do you believe God created anything by accident?

**So God created mankind in his own image,
in the image of God he created them;
male and female he created them.
That is why a man leaves his father and mother
and is united to his wife, and
they become one flesh.** GENESIS 1:27; 2:24

God designed nature to teach us his wisdom and power. God designed our consciences to teach us his holiness. God designed sex to teach us . . .?

If all God had in mind with our sexuality was procreation, he could have had a man take off his little finger and a woman take off hers. They put them in a glass of water and stir and she drinks it and becomes pregnant. Then they both grow back their little fingers. He could have done it that way. Or he could have made us like fish. She drops her eggs, he swims by and drops his sperm, and ne'er the twain shall meet. He could have done that.

Instead, he designed us for oneness, one flesh. The Spirit inspired Paul to explain further that this oneness is more than just sex; it's becoming one (1 Corinthians 6:16). A husband and wife making love show each other and God that the two are one. British poet Charles Williams captured it as only a poet can: "Love you? I am you."

Pornographers would like us to believe that sex is nothing more than doing what genitals do. That's the opposite of God's design. Sort of makes you pity those who fall for it. It doesn't come close to the reality for which God designed our bodies: oneness.

- Take the time to individually prepare to tell your spouse the time(s) you feel most "one" with him or her.

Pray that you see in God's gift of sexuality a tremendous opportunity to demonstrate your oneness.

Enjoy Sexual Intimacy

God uses the same word to describe a husband and wife making love as he uses to describe himself. Surprised?

Adam *knew* Eve his wife; and she conceived. GENESIS 4:1 (KJV)

**"I will give them a heart to *know* me,
that I am the LORD."** JEREMIAH 24:7

Adam knew his wife like no one else knew her, and likewise, Eve knew her husband. He let himself be known by her; she let herself be known by him. Sex is about knowing. The Lord used the same word to describe himself and our relationship with him. Christianity is about being known by God and knowing him.

If sex is purely physical, it's likely to become stale or boring. If sex is purely spiritual, you're falling for bad theology. God made our bodies as much as our souls. He made some parts of the body with no other purpose than pleasure. Why would he make us the way he did if he didn't intend us to enjoy sexual intimacy? It's his gift to you.

This is how to put porn to shame and see it for what it is: a cheap substitute for the real thing. Don't make sex about the release of endorphins and enkephalins. Make sex about knowing and letting your spouse know you. Then your sex life is natural and focused on each other. God's plan for sexual intimacy doesn't take the fun out of it; it makes it more fun. When you know this, you stop searching *Cosmopolitan* or *Men's Health* for the way to make sex better. If it's about knowing your spouse, it's already very, very good.

- Tell your spouse the part(s) of your body that bring you the most pleasure.

Pray that you make the connection between your sexual pleasure and knowing each other.

Enjoy Sexual Intimacy

That fire in your furnace or fireplace is not a threat to you. Let it go beyond its boundary, though, and you have much to fear.

**Moses and Aaron then went into the tent of meeting . . .
and the glory of the Lord appeared to all the people.
Fire came out from the presence of the Lord and consumed
the burnt offering. . . . Aaron's sons Nadab and Abihu took
their censers, put fire in them and added incense; and they
offered unauthorized fire before the Lord, contrary to
his command. So fire came out from the presence of
the Lord and consumed them, and they died
before the Lord. LEVITICUS 9:23–10:2**

The Lord told his people how to use the things in the Tent of Meeting and not to bring in their own unauthorized, or strange, unholy fire. The Bible doesn't explain this event further, but the message was clear: God is serious about the sacred nature of meeting him.

God put boundaries around the sacred fire of sexuality to tell us, "This is a precious gift, and you can't just use it any way you want." Jesus redeemed your body, including your sexuality. That's what makes it special. His major boundary is this: restricted to a husband and wife. That's the only God-pleasing context for this fire.

In the Bible, it sounds like this: "That is why . . . they become one flesh" (Genesis 2:24). In our world, it sounds like this: "I am with you until one of us lays the other into the arms of God. Then, good or bad, we'll figure it out. We'll stick to each other."

- Discuss actions a husband and wife can take to safeguard the boundaries around sex.

Pray that you always enjoy the fire of sexual intimacy within the bounds of your marriage.

☀ SUMMER ☀

Forgive Each Other

The opposite of forgiveness is revenge. Revenge is the poison pill I swallow, hoping it will make the other person sick. It seldom does. Ironically, the cost of your forgiveness did more than make Jesus sick; it killed him.

[Jesus said,] "Father, if you are willing, take this cup from me; yet not my will, but yours be done." LUKE 22:42

When Jesus looked into that cup, he saw more than his death. He saw *the* death we all deserved, and then he drank it to the dregs. God doesn't just call you forgiven; he pays for it.

Forgiveness always costs, but you can't have a marriage without it. You married a sinner, and so did your spouse. So you both will always need to be prepared to pay the price and forgive your spouse for the sake of your marriage.

Consider three actions of forgiveness: (1) When you forgive, you give up certain things: the right to get even, to get what you deserve, to hurt as you've been hurt. (2) You give notice to the one who has sinned against you what you are forgiving. It's easier to remain silent, but that encourages no change in the one who sinned against you. (3) You give gifts. The receiver doesn't deserve it, and the giver doesn't demand anything for it. This is love that loves with no reason or guarantee it will be loved in return. It's doing the loving thing, even when you don't feel like it—like Jesus did for you when he drank the cup.

- Recall how Jesus completed the three actions of forgiveness.

- Which of the three actions of forgiveness is most difficult for you? Why?

Pray that you appreciate the price Jesus paid for your forgiveness and learn from him how to forgive.

Forgive Each Other

Every marriage is cross-cultural. You may be of the same ethnicity, but one of you opened gifts on Christmas Eve, the other on Christmas Day. One of you kept the kitchen trash bin in the pantry, the other under the sink. Those differences can not only cause conflict but also the need for forgiveness.

Forgive as the Lord forgave you. COLOSSIANS 3:13

Sin is one of the differences between God and us. In Colossians 2, Paul told us how the Lord forgave it: He took the record of our sins and nailed it to the cross. Only the pierced hands and feet of God could take away our sin. Now we take the vertical forgiveness we receive from God and bend it horizontally toward our spouse.

Opening Christmas gifts and storing trash are just the beginning. List other possible conflicts in marriage due to differences between a husband and wife, whether major or mundane. Don't stop until you get to ten items.

When we don't manage those conflicts well, we will need to forgive. Forgiving love involves two people doing two things: asking for forgiveness and granting forgiveness. Asking for forgiveness might sound like "I was wrong" or "I'm sorry" or "I don't ever want to hurt you like that again" or "Will you forgive me for . . ." Granting forgiveness might sound like "I forgive you and I close this issue" or "I forgive you for . . ." or "I forgive you because God forgives me." Such statements aren't formulas; they're attitudes of the heart, like the Lord's heart for you.

- We call Psalms 6, 32, 38, 51, 102, 130, and 143 the penitential psalms. Choose one to read together, and then tell each other one thing you learned from it about asking for or granting forgiveness.

Pray that you become better at asking for and granting forgiveness.

Forgive Each Other

Jacob ran for his life away from his brother, Esau. Before they met again, two decades later, Jacob sent Esau a gift of hundreds of animals to say, "I'm sorry about the whole birthright thing." Esau tried to decline the gift. Jacob insisted:

"If I have found favor in your eyes, accept this gift from me. For to see your face is like seeing the face of God." GENESIS 33:10

Maybe Jacob knew it would be harder for Esau to forgive him than Esau knew. Esau said it was enough just to see his brother again. But in taking his brother's birthright, Jacob had broken a sacred trust. He wouldn't take his brother's forgiveness for granted. Instead, he valued his brother's forgiveness as much as God's forgiveness.

Marriage is a sacred trust. When you stood before the altar, or on the beach, or in the barn, you made two promises. You made the first promise facing the pastor, not each other, because it was a promise to God to live as husband and wife until death. You made the second promise facing each other, to take each other as husband and wife. Your marriage is both sacred and practical.

It doesn't take theology to discern how important forgiveness is in a relationship. Forgiveness brings a practical kind of peace and stability. But, oh, your marriage is a sacred thing. When you forgive each other, you're showing each other the type of grace God has shown you. Seeing your spouse forgive you is "like seeing the face of God."

- Recall as many details as possible about the time you spoke the two promises of marriage. Listen to or watch a recording if possible.

Pray that you value both the practical and the sacred nature of your marriage.

☀ SUMMER ☀

Build a Life Together

Boundaries help to create and sustain rituals and traditions in our marriages.

If a man has recently married, he must not be sent to war or have any other duty laid on him. For one year he is to be free to stay at home and bring happiness to the wife he has married. DEUTERONOMY 24:5

That must have been a powerful recruitment strategy both for military service and for marriage! The same Lord who instituted marriage put boundaries around it. When his people succeed in marriage, they glorify him and witness to others about him. The boundaries are good for us.

Nothing can be special if it's constantly interrupted. Family dinner can become less special if you take phone calls, look at text messages, or watch TV. Lunch together becomes an opportunity for insult if you check your messages.

My father was occasionally interrupted by a phone call from someone at work during our family dinner. That was about it. Today, work, friends, family, and feeds can ping us a dozen times during any hour—if we let them. Probably like never before, we need to create boundaries of our own choosing. No one will hold you to it; it's up to you.

- What do other couples do to protect their time together?

- Tell your spouse, "I wish you were less distracted by _____ when we're together." Don't get defensive at what you hear. You don't have to agree; just listen. Your spouse told you something that took courage and that he or she is convinced would help you build a life together. Thank God for what you heard.

Pray that you see through the interruptions and distractions from each other.

☀ SUMMER ☀

Build a Life Together

Building a life together doesn't just happen. It takes work.

Jesus Christ laid down his life for us. . . . Dear children, let us not love with words or speech but with actions and in truth. 1 JOHN 3:16,18

John reached back to the crucifixion and pointed ahead to your marriage. We're fallen and won't always get it right; we'll act selfishly. Later, John reminded us, "If our hearts condemn us, we know that God is greater than our hearts" (1 John 3:20). His love led him to make the ultimate payment for sin, not with words but with actions. No love is greater.

Train yourself to look at your spouse as one for whom Jesus Christ laid down his life. Let that view shape what you're willing to invest in him or her. Ask yourself, *What actions will now show my love to my spouse?* We build a life together by our words and by our actions. That takes work.

Just like it takes energy to do most anything important, it takes energy to value your spouse, to value being together, and to connect intentionally. When you put energy into your marriage, you're more likely to be happy with each other. Of course, not everything will go your way, but it won't matter as much. It's how you'll bring glory to God and joy to each other.

- Recall one thing your spouse did that required attention, work, and energy above and beyond. It could be something small (you put a card in my suitcase) or something big (you came away from your work to watch the Academy Awards together).

- Determine one thing you'll do tomorrow that won't cost money to show your spouse you're investing in your marriage.

Pray that you put your limited energy into that which promises a good return: your marriage.

Build a Life Together

Making a decision is often difficult because choosing one option means not choosing other options. And we like our options.

In your relationships with one another, have the same mindset as Christ Jesus: Who, being in very nature God, did not consider equality with God something to be used to his own advantage; rather, he made himself nothing. PHILIPPIANS 2:5-7

Jesus was all in. He gave up the choice to stay in glory, enjoy worship as God, and keep all his power as God. Those were attractive alternatives to descending into poverty, being mocked, and setting aside most of his power as God. He made those choices only on account of his desire for you. We respond to Jesus by giving up some choices too. We daily give up the choice to sin. We give up creating new idols and living for ourselves.

Jesus gave his all because he wants all of you. Then he wants you to turn around and give all of yourself to your spouse. To be all in for your spouse means you make time for him or her before other things gobble it up.

When we commit to something, we give up some options. When you bought a Subaru, you gave up the option of a Chevy. Choosing one means giving up the other. When you decided to get married and build a life together, you gave up some things too. Sure, you gave up the big things like a different spouse or the life of a single man or woman. But what things do you give up now to be all in for your spouse?

- Name activities you do that show you put your spouse ahead of other things.

Pray that you put God first and your spouse second.

Trust

When you decided to marry, you didn't just choose each other. God chose you for each other (Mark 10:9). Let his choice move you to wear a kind of clothing that builds trust.

As God's chosen people, holy and dearly loved, clothe yourselves with compassion, kindness, humility, gentleness and patience. COLOSSIANS 3:12

The Lord compliments you by calling you to develop the same characteristic that is his nature: kindness. Paul wrote, "When the kindness and love of God our Savior appeared, he saved us" (Titus 3:4,5). Paul called Jesus the kindness of God. Now God calls you to develop kindness.

Compassion feels and wants to act; kindness acts. You've seen the bumper sticker about random *acts* of kindness. Kindness is something you do. If you're familiar with *The Five Love Languages* by Gary Chapman, you know about it. If you discover that your spouse feels more loved by your filling the car up with gas than by receiving expensive gifts, you just saved a ton of money! More than that, you've shown that you're paying attention. You're speaking his or her language. It's work, but that's what it takes to build trust.

- Agree on one time, other than his crucifixion, when Jesus demonstrated kindness.

- Explain why kindness builds trust.

- Tell each other how you complete this sentence: "I think one of the kindest things you have done for me is . . ." If you need some time to think and prepare for that conversation, agree to start your next devotion time together with it.

Pray that you repent of the times you could have shown kindness but didn't, thank Jesus for his kindness to you, and ask him to help you learn from your conversation about kindness.

Trust

Have you ever greeted each other, "Good morning, holy one"? Try it tomorrow morning. God says you can.

As God's chosen people, holy and dearly loved, clothe yourselves with compassion, kindness, humility, gentleness and patience. COLOSSIANS 3:12

Before Paul tells you to put on clothes that build trust, he calls you holy. When Martin Luther wrote a book to help parents teach their children the truths of God's Word, he explained the First Petition of the Lord's Prayer, "Hallowed be your name," this way: "God's name is certainly holy by itself, but we pray in this petition that we too may keep it holy." There's the difference between God's holiness and ours. He is holy all by himself; we are not. That's why you bristled at the thought of greeting your spouse, "Good morning, holy one." You both know you're not, but you are holy by your faith in Jesus. Try to see each other that way.

Knowing we need God's holiness brings humility. Humility is the conviction that you are here to use the gifts God has given you for the benefit of others, first for your spouse. What do people say you're good at? Come on, now is no time for false modesty. What do you like to do? How are you using those gifts and abilities to serve your spouse? Your answer may be encouraging or convicting. But do it and you'll build trust.

- Agree on a time, other than his crucifixion, when Jesus demonstrated humility.

- Explain why humility would build trust in a marriage.

- None of us are humble. The best we can say is we're proud people pursuing humility. Tell each other one person you consider advanced in his or her pursuit of humility.

Pray with thanksgiving to Jesus for his humility and that you might learn from those who display humility.

Trust

Many describe Jesus as gentle. If I were to ask people to describe how you treat each other, would their first response be, "With gentleness"?

As God's chosen people, holy and dearly loved, clothe yourselves with compassion, kindness, humility, gentleness and patience. COLOSSIANS 3:12

Jesus was gentle with a woman ostracized for five failed marriages and with Peter who swore he didn't even know Jesus. There's gentle Jesus. He was tempted to be disgusted with the woman at the well and to curse Peter on the spot. But he didn't. There's saving Jesus. Rather than shaming you or damning you, he lives and dies for you. He gives you repentance and faith and promises. "He does not treat us as our sins deserve . . . so great is his love for those who fear him" (Psalm 103:10,11).

Let Jesus' gentleness with you influence the way you speak to each other today. If gentleness describes your daily discourse, praise God. If not, work on it. Women, find a wife who demonstrates gentleness, take her to coffee, and learn. When you're tempted to roll your eyes at her gentleness, remember Jesus' gentleness. Men, find a husband who demonstrates gentleness. Find a way to get together with him: Volunteer with him at church or ask his opinion about something else (most men don't want to talk about gentleness). Learn from him. The best way to learn gentleness is from a gentle person: Jesus first, then a gentle person in your life.

- Recall two more examples of Jesus being gentle.

- Explain why, in your opinion, gentleness builds trust.

- Tell each other one time when you noticed gentleness in the other.

Pray that Jesus impresses you with his gentleness, opens your eyes to see it in others, and helps you be gentler with your spouse.

☀ SUMMER ☀

Pursue Friendship

She said on their 60th anniversary, "He was so shy I knew he'd never ask me to marry him, so I asked him, 'Do you want to get married?' He said, 'I suppose so. Do you?' " With a chuckle, he quipped, "We're better friends now than we were then." Don't you want your spouse to say that? Find the benefits of a friend in these verses.

> **There was a man all alone; he had neither son nor brother. There was no end to his toil, yet his eyes were not content with his wealth. "For whom am I toiling," he asked, "and why am I depriving myself of enjoyment?" This too is meaningless—a miserable business! Two are better than one, because they have a good return for their labor: If either of them falls down, one can help the other up. But pity anyone who falls and has no one to help them up. Also, if two lie down together, they will keep warm. But how can one keep warm alone? Though one may be overpowered, two can defend themselves. A cord of three strands is not quickly broken.** ECCLESIASTES 4:8-12

According to Solomon, if you pursue friendship, you can expect the benefits of companionship, productivity, support, warmth, and protection. You might add that a friend is someone to relax with, open up to, count on, and do fun things with. A friend is happy to see you and doesn't have immediate plans for your improvement.

People who have friends, especially one really good one, do better in almost every way in life. Is that what you're pursuing together?

- Tell each other two things you most value about your friendship.

Pray that you are better friends at the end of your marriage than you are today.

 **☀ SUMMER ☀**

Pursue Friendship

Friends open up to each other. Even if you don't wear your heart on your sleeve, you occasionally reveal yourself to your best friend.

"I no longer call you servants, because a servant does not know his master's business. Instead, I have called you friends, for everything that I learned from my Father I have made known to you." JOHN 15:15

Jesus is your friend! What evidence does he present to prove that? He has disclosed the deep things of God to you. He made known to us some things that are hard to hear. He rebukes us as he did Peter, "You have in mind the concerns of God, but merely human concerns" (Matthew 16:23). But some things are gloriously welcome news: "I have called you friends." Such is the benefit of Jesus' sacrifice and God's grace that is yours because of it.

What gets in the way of your friendship with each other?

Is it time? You made time for each other when you were dating. The pace of life and your responsibilities have probably changed, but it's still a matter of choices and priorities. Schedule friend time.

Is it your conversation? Do you talk more politely to people at work than to each other? How odd is that? Friends talk about sports, politics, fun things, plans, God's presence, etc. Sadly, married people can talk more about problems than those things: the problems with the kids, the house, the car, the finances, etc. To pursue friendship, talk like friends. Don't just focus on the problems. Agree to set them aside for a bit.

Discuss together what you can do to:

- Make time for each other.

- Talk like friends.

Pray that you treasure Jesus' friendship and pursue your friendship.

Pursue Friendship

Some have observed that we tend to become more optimistic with age. So let's leverage that likelihood to pursue our friendship together.

[Jesus said,] "First take the plank out of your eye, and then you will see clearly to remove the speck from your brother's eye." LUKE 6:42

Jesus specialized in calling out hypocrisy. We tend to hide it; he exposed it. He did so not to embarrass or shame us but to heal us. Healing comes from repentance: "God, I see the same fault in me. Forgive me and help me overcome it."

When you see a speck in your spouse's eye, you may be presuming you can do what God has said we cannot: read people's minds and hearts. Usually, we err on the negative side. Good things may be happening, but you might not recognize the positive in anything he or she does. The more stressed the situation, the worse it can get. It might sound like "You did that because you . . ." It's judgmental, it's hurtful, and it kills friendship.

Instead of reading your spouse's heart, take inventory of your own heart. Then repent, serve, and pray for your spouse. Those steps will only build your friendship.

The next time you're only seeing the bad in your spouse:

- Ask yourself, *Is this really negative behavior or just my negative interpretation?*

- Ask yourself, *What evidence contradicts my negative interpretation?*

- Give him or her the benefit of the doubt.

- Ask Jesus to remove the plank from your eye.

Pray that you see the plank in your own eye, repent, and receive healing.

 **❀ FALL ❀**

Communicate With Each Other

Hearing is involuntary. Sound waves hit your eardrum, vibrations enter your cochlea, and your brain does the rest. You can't help it, really. Listening is different than simply hearing. Listening requires conscious effort, understanding, and interpretation. When God hears, he listens.

In my distress I called to the LORD; I cried to my God for help. From his temple he heard my voice; my cry came before him, into his ears. PSALM 18:6

David wrote this psalm when his enemies threatened. He talked to God. God understood his need and responded. David knew his life depended on God not just hearing but *listening* and responding in grace. He wasn't disappointed. The sin that would block your prayers from God's ears has been removed. He loves to listen to you too.

Good communication with your spouse requires more than just hearing. It requires listening and that requires work: attention, effort, understanding, follow-up questions, and interpreting what it means to the speaker, not just to you.

If listening were easy, we'd probably all be good at it. But we can all become better at it. We learn about it every time we pray. These conversations will help too. Don't rush them. Take your time and listen to each other's input.

- Identify three *internal* obstacles to listening that are inside you (e.g., judging, defensiveness, anticipating, interrupting, etc.).

- Identify three *external* obstacles to listening that exist outside you (e.g., noise, frantic pace, etc.).

- For each obstacle, discuss what you could do to overcome it.

Pray that you glorify God by trusting his promise to listen when you pray, that you become more aware of and overcome the obstacles to listening to your spouse.

Communicate With Each Other

Playwright George Bernard Shaw said, "England and America are two countries separated by a common language." Have you ever thought the same of men and women?

Male and female he created them. GENESIS 1:27

On the sixth day of creation, God crowned all that he had made with a man and a woman, equally sinless, gifted, valuable to the Creator, and given different roles to complement and support each other. After the fall into sin, they were equally sinful, gifted, valuable to the God who promised a Savior, and still with different roles to complement and support each other. It's been that way ever since.

God created men and women to be distinct. For example, the left hemisphere of the brain, responsible for speech, is more fully developed in baby girls. The right hemisphere, responsible for visual and spatial skills, is more fully developed in baby boys. Not more or less valuable, just different.

Here's another example. When your wife says, "I have nothing to wear," what does she mean? When your husband says, "I have nothing to wear," what does he mean? Not better or worse, but very different!

What you discover in the following activity may not be accurate for you, but generalities exist because they are generally true. Privately prepare two responses to each of the following three instructions. Then tell each other your answers. Don't get defensive or angry. Ask questions to better understand. You speak the same language, so this should be easy, right?

- How does the communication of the opposite sex generally frustrate you?
- What do you wish the opposite sex would do specifically to change their communication with you?
- How can you help each other overcome these challenges specifically in your marriage?

Pray that you value the distinctions God made between men and women.

Communicate With Each Other

Perfect communication doesn't exist anymore, but that wasn't always true. There was a time when a man experienced perfect communication with God.

The Lord God said, "It is not good for the man to be alone. I will make a helper suitable for him." GENESIS 2:18

Adam was in direct communication with God, but he was alone. God's solution? Eve. In marriage, two become one, and each one lives to glorify the other. But we may do that in different ways, even painfully obvious different ways.

In most marriages, one spouse is an "expander" who looks for ways to expand the communication territory, who talks to relate. Often the other spouse is a "contractor" who looks for ways to shorten communication.

The expander saw a batter hit by a pitch and told her friend, "Can you imagine how his wife must have felt? He must have wondered on the way to the dugout how this would affect his career. I'm so glad my husband doesn't play professional baseball." The contractor told his friend, "A guy got hit by a pitch."

Neither is wrong. Both are built by God and gifted by the Spirit. Each can reflect to the other the love Jesus has shown them both by building a bridge to the other. Here are four ways to build that bridge. Determine which bridge(s) *you* want to build. Tell each other which one(s), why, and how you'll work on it.

1. Talk more or listen better.

2. Dump the details.

3. Tell you what I'd like from you at the beginning of a conversation I bring up.

4. Learn to tell you how I feel about something.

Pray that you don't expect perfect communication with each other but that you continually work together to improve your communication.

❀ FALL ❀

Appreciate Each Other

You're either moving toward enhancing the glory of your spouse or degrading your spouse. That's not new.

[Adam] said, "The woman you put here with me—she gave me some fruit from the tree, and I ate it." GENESIS 3:12

Ever since the fall into sin, our fallen nature drives us to blame others as the problem. It's difficult to feel affection for someone who's pointing an accusing finger at you.

Scripture continues unfolding the same marriage drama. Jacob worshiped Rachel in a way that could only hurt (Genesis 29–30). Worship corrupts the one worshiped and makes the one worshiping blind and needy. Samson used Delilah; Delilah used Samson (Judges 16). They were ancient friends with benefits. Michal shamed David by refusing to share his joy (2 Samuel 6). King Xerxes treated Queen Vashti like an object (Esther 1).

And on it goes, until Jesus receives in his body the degrading actions of all humans of all time. He bears the penalty we deserve so he can share with us the glory of God.

You've seen other married people degrade each other by their words or actions. The following exercise isn't for gossip or for agreeing or disagreeing with your spouse. It's to learn what your spouse feels is degrading so you can avoid it.

- Recall a time you've seen someone degrade his or her spouse. You don't have to name names; it might help not to. Don't play devil's advocate. Just listen carefully and say thank you. And make a mental note.

Pray that you thank Jesus for forgiving us at the cross and cleansing us of all guilt for every time we have degraded each other. Ask him to help you see what your spouse is telling you and learn from it.

Appreciate Each Other

Everything in the Bible is written for our learning, but not everything was written for our imitating. Examples of couples degrading each other abound. But what would it look like to enhance the glory of your spouse?

Boaz took Ruth and she became his wife. RUTH 4:13

Boaz saw Ruth's need. He provided her with food and positioned her to make friends. He gave her a job and set her up to succeed in it. Ruth knew she was in a vulnerable position, but she also knew she could trust Boaz, and she did. Boaz prayed for her, acknowledged her kindness, and showed respect to her. They enhanced each other's glory. The book of Ruth is a great read, and it's only four chapters!

Most important, Matthew includes Ruth in Jesus' genealogy. Through the marriage of Boaz and Ruth, the Lord provided the human ancestry of his Son our Savior.

You've admired married people who have by their words or actions enhanced the glory of their spouse; they made them look good to others. The following exercise isn't to put others on an inappropriate pedestal. It's to learn what your spouse feels is beautiful in a relationship. Why would that matter? So you can show your appreciation in similar ways.

- Recall a time you've seen someone honor or respect his or her spouse. You could tell the person wanted to make the other look good. You don't have to name names; it might help not to. Just listen carefully and say, "Tell me more about that." And make a mental note.

Pray that you thank God for sending his Son through people like Boaz and Ruth and ask him to help you find ways to honor and enhance the glory of your spouse.

❋ FALL ❋

Appreciate Each Other

Our verse for today didn't become a common mealtime prayer by accident. We find in it a way to express our appreciation for God's qualities.

**Give thanks to the LORD, for he is good;
his love endures forever.** PSALM 118:1

God's goodness doesn't change when we fail to appreciate who he is or what he does. At best, we tend to take the blessings he gives for granted. At worst, we claim credit for them. This verse brings us back to reality: We have because he provides. He provides because of his goodness and mercy.

At a staff meeting, workers were asked to name important qualities that help an employee function best in the current times. They produced a whiteboard full of characteristics. Then each worker was told to point at someone else and pair up. The assignment: Tell about a time you've seen that person demonstrate one of the qualities on the board in the workplace. The only rule was you can't disagree. You can only say thank you. The simple exercise produced profound results: a new sense of being appreciated. It's not a raise in pay, but it's almost as good.

People may line up to criticize your spouse, but not as many express their appreciation. When you appreciate your spouse's qualities, you get something money can't buy: friendship.

- Recall a time your spouse did or said something that made your face light up. Plan a date specifically to tell each other. Prepare. Make notes to help you remember details and words you want to use.

Pray that you recall the Lord's goodness and love and thank him for his qualities. Pray that you find little or big ways to tell your spouse how you appreciate him or her.

Manage Conflict

Ask a newly engaged couple, "Where are you two incompatible?" and you might hear a cheerful "Nowhere!" But what will their answer be after planning the wedding? After years of marriage? Whether we always see it or not, we're incompatible for many reasons.

I know that good itself does not dwell in me, that is, in my sinful nature. For I have the desire to do what is good, but I cannot carry it out. ROMANS 7:18

When you add together our sinful nature, Satan, and the fallen world we live in, we might start to wonder how we can ever be compatible. It starts with this: Jesus solved our incompatibility with God. It took nothing less than his perfect life and his innocent death, but he solved it for you.

Conflicts in marriage arise for those and other reasons too numerous to list, but here's one: we change. You're not the same person your spouse married. Neither is your spouse the same. You've both changed physically, socially, mentally, and psychologically. That's one fallacy about living together before marriage. Some think, *Then we'll know each other.* Yeah, but what about after 5 years of changes or 25 years of changes?

Incompatibility is more about *us* than it is about *you.* You both change, but you can stay connected even through the changes. Start with this: See your incompatibility as grounds for marriage, not separation. Your differences allow you to love and accept each other as Christ loves and accepts you.

- Privately write three ways you've changed since you got married (only one can be physical). When you're done, show each other what you've written.

- Discuss what you've learned from this activity and agree on two implications this has for your marriage.

Pray that you see your incompatibility as opportunities to put your spouse, your spouse's needs, and your spouse's happiness ahead of your own.

Manage Conflict

If you've been using this book, this isn't the first time you've read: "We cannot *not have conflict." The repetition and the double negative are intentional.*

No one will be declared righteous in God's sight by the works of the law; rather, through the law we become conscious of our sin. But now apart from the law the righteousness of God has been made known, to which the Law and the Prophets testify. This righteousness is given through faith in Jesus Christ to all who believe. ROMANS 3:20-22

The apostle Paul made clear the greatest conflict we have is sin. The sinful nature we inherited from our parents and the sins we commit are our conflict with God. The works of the law will never solve our conflict with God; Jesus' righteousness already has. Faith in him brings with it credit for his righteous life and his death as payment for your conflict: sin. That's Christian faith.

Acknowledge that and gain a different perspective on conflicts with your spouse. It may not solve those conflicts, but it means you know how: the cross. Christian spouses start managing their conflicts at a different point. We start at the finish line. Our worst conflict, conflict with a holy God, is resolved. Then we back up to manage our conflicts with each other.

- Individually, use Romans 3:20–22 to write three different things God did to solve your conflict with him.

- Compare what you've written. Celebrate each similar response you have. Ask each other to clarify answers that are different: "What made you think of that?"

Pray that you take to heart the greatest solution to the greatest conflict: Jesus' righteousness given to you by faith.

❄ FALL ❄

Manage Conflict

Sometimes the cause of a conflict isn't sin. It might be about something good.

What causes fights and quarrels among you? Don't they come from your desires that battle within you? You desire but do not have, so you kill. You covet but you cannot get what you want, so you quarrel and fight. You do not have because you do not ask God. When you ask, you do not receive, because you ask with wrong motives, that you may spend what you get on your pleasures. JAMES 4:1-3

It's possible to want something good but in a sinful way. James and John wanted cabinet positions. Peter wanted to stand up to Jesus' enemies in the Garden of Gethsemane. Thomas wanted visible proof of the resurrection. Those weren't bad motives, but Jesus could see their motives and calmly redirected their desires to the good of God's kingdom, not their own good. He does the same for your desires.

We'll never be able to look into someone's heart and see motives, but we can look into our own hearts. Conflicts often come from one or both of you not feeling valued. When you don't feel valued, you tend to resist and react negatively. When you know your spouse values your opinions and beliefs, the atmosphere stays safe even when you disagree.

- Find as many reasons as you can in the James passage above for our wanting good things in sinful ways.

- Fill in the blank and tell each other, "When we disagree, but you respond to me with _____ (e.g., kindness, respect, tenderness, understanding, etc.), I feel valued."

Pray that you look in yourself for the reason you have a conflict. Where it is sin, repent. Where it is not sin, ask God to purify your motives and help you to value your spouse.

Serve Each Other

Moviemakers know the draw of the story of a spouse caring for a dying mate.
Think Love Story *or* The Notebook. *What movie comes to your mind?*

[Jesus said,] "Not so with you. Instead, whoever wants
to become great among you must be your servant, and
whoever wants to be first must be slave of all." MARK 10:43,44

Jesus became the slave of all, even of those who didn't want
him to serve them. Through his whole life and even at his death,
Jesus made it clear he served people who didn't want him. I recall
an atrium conversation after a church service. A guest remarked,
"Hasn't Christianity moved past the demand for blood atonement
by an angry God? I don't need a Savior like that." Jesus became a
slave even for that person. Jesus served him with his life, just like
he served you.

You love him for it. You show it by the way you love your
spouse. Your care for your spouse, long before either of you is
dying but certainly when you are, is a powerful testimony to your
Savior's care for you.

- Take the time now to complete this sentence five
  different ways:

  To serve your spouse means . . .

- Tell each other two things:

  1. One thing I most appreciate about the way you serve
     me is . . .

  2. What one thing can I do to serve you?

Pray that the good news of how Jesus has served you washes over
you, impresses you, and moves you to want to serve your spouse.

Serve Each Other

In 1992, Dr. Gary Chapman published The Five Love Languages. *It's not the gospel, but through it, millions have learned how to better respond to the gospel by serving their spouses.*

God spoke all these words. EXODUS 20:1

God communicates to us through words. He doesn't speak in high-pitched whale sounds or a cow's lowing. He uses words. He uses words to convict us of our sin, comfort us with the record of Jesus' saving work, and guide us through daily and lifelong decisions. He speaks our language so we can know his love.

Dr. Chapman teaches that your spouse best receives love through one or more of five love languages. Your task is to discover your spouse's language and speak it. Find an online listing or buy the book to discover your love language. That's the easy part. The hard part is then forgetting your love language and remembering to speak the language your spouse speaks. Here's one: Words of Affirmation.

Does your spouse feel most loved by words of affirmation? Then work on giving verbal compliments, speaking encouraging words, building a vocabulary of kind words, and asking for grace to speak humble words. But be careful. If the motive is love, you won't speak it to manipulate. That's no one's love language.

- Determine how each sentence could either be encouragement or manipulation.
    1. "Go ahead, honey, take that online course in accounting."
    2. "I'm encouraging him to lose weight, but he's not taking it well."
    3. "If you want to do this, you'll succeed. I'm behind you 100 percent."
    4. "This is a fantastic article; you should publish it."
    5. "I can tell this is important to you. Maybe now isn't the time, though."

Pray that you serve your spouse with words of affirmation.

❀ FALL ❀

Serve Each Other

The average US citizen lives about 80 years. Subtract your current age from 80. Multiply that times 365. That's about how many days you have left. When we give attention to each other, we're giving a portion of those finite minutes. We might spend them sitting at a restaurant or on the couch. Another of Dr. Chapman's love languages is Quality Time.

Our days may come to seventy years, or eighty, if our strength endures; yet the best of them are but trouble and sorrow, for they quickly pass, and we fly away. PSALM 90:10

The psalmist was brutal but honest. So was Jesus. He lived a righteous life every day because we could not. He didn't sugarcoat our guilt, but he bore its ugly weight on his cross. Jesus was equally honest about our future: living with him forever, where our days will have no trouble or sorrow.

Marriage at its best is wonderful and at its worst can be deeply disappointing. But the time available to work toward the former and away from the latter is limited. Does your spouse feel especially loved when you spend quality time with him or her?

Quality time doesn't require you staring into each other's eyes for hours, but it does mean giving your attention to the same thing together. Watching TV, not so much. Walking together, participating in a hobby or game together, or using the same Bible reading plan are some options. The central aspect is togetherness.

- Tell each other a time when you gave your attention to the same thing together—a time that showed your spouse cared about you, that you enjoyed and would like to do again.

- Recall an activity your spouse has mentioned doing together—and plan for it.

Pray that you value the time you have together.

🍁 FALL 🍁

Spiritual Intimacy

The COVID-19 pandemic taught us something about church. We can hear God's Word virtually and even watch the preacher, but something is missing when we don't meet together. That thing is fellowship.

Let us consider how we may spur one another on toward love and good deeds, not giving up meeting together, as some are in the habit of doing, but encouraging one another—and all the more as you see the Day approaching. HEBREWS 10:24,25

The local congregation is the hope of the world but only because Jesus is its message. The message is hope for sinners and confidence in the future for saints. We need both; according to the Bible, it's best to share such gifts together.

In this fallen world, there's something wrong with every church. That's because we're in it. When we come to worship, Satan will do his best to get us to be critical of the service, distracted, and judgmental of others. No wonder some preferred couch worship during the pandemic. In some ways, it's easier, but the point of worship isn't to be easy. It is to be one way we encourage each other. For that to happen, we need to encounter God's presence together.

Not every husband and wife attend the same church, but if it were possible, every couple would. You can debrief together, discuss the sermon, recall a favorite phrase in a hymn, and even laugh at something humorous. You can use what you heard to encourage each other and witness to others. If you don't attend the same church, is it time to revisit the possibility? If you do, is it because of the doctrine, the programs, the music, the style of the service, the nurture ministries, the outreach mind-set, the sermons, or something else?

- Tell each other one thing that you especially enjoy about your church.

Pray that you find joy in encouraging each other through your church.

✿ FALL ✿

Spiritual Intimacy

Every living thing is growing. If it stops growing, it's dead. The same is true of your faith. What is your plan for spiritual growth?

All Scripture is God-breathed and is useful for teaching, rebuking, correcting and training in righteousness, so that the servant of God may be thoroughly equipped for every good work. 2 TIMOTHY 3:16,17

If you buy a new car and neglect all routine maintenance, it shouldn't surprise you how often it's in the shop. If you get married and neglect all God teaches you in his Word, it shouldn't surprise you when you end up in counseling or divorce court. You neglected the One who designed your marriage and promised to bless you in it. Pay attention to God's Word and your problems might not disappear, but you'll be equipped to handle them in a way that brings glory to God and joy to your home.

Do you find it easier to first develop a personal devotional life based on God's Word and then establish a routine for your devotions together? Or is the reverse true for you? Most agree that it's easiest if you make it a habit. Establish your own ritual around it (When do you do it? Who reads? Who prays? Do you light a candle? etc.). You'll still be drawn away by good things that need your attention, but at least you won't be fooled by silly, less important things.

What devotional resource will you use? You'll explore that in the following devotion. For now, let's explore how you got to this book and what you're experiencing through it.

- Tell each other one thing you each appreciate about your current couple's devotional ritual.

- Tell each other one thing you'd like to change about your current couple's devotional ritual.

Pray that you commit together to continuing your devotional ritual.

FALL

Spiritual Intimacy

❖

Some couples have a happy marriage without faith in Jesus. They've learned to be decent, and that's a good thing. But your faith in Jesus not only connects you to God's riches but also gives your marriage a higher purpose. You're married to glorify him together. You are for each other a picture of God's unconditional love.

Faith comes from hearing the message, and the message is heard through the word about Christ. ROMANS 10:17

Notice Paul's sentence construction: "faith comes from hearing." That's very passive. Faith doesn't come from reaching up to heaven and grabbing it. It doesn't come from generating an emotional response deep in your heart. If faith came from such actions, we'd get some credit for it. But hearing? It's hard to be more passive. Sit there. Let it hit your ears. Receive it. A beautiful bonus about God's way of distributing faith: you can do this together.

Which devotional resources are you curious about? Do some research; some are free, and some cost a little but are well worth it. Christian publishers offer hundreds of devotional resources. Because of doctrinal differences, sometimes subtle, you should read them with discernment. That's not bad, but if you'd rather not make that your purpose or challenge, then choose one from your own fellowship. You're using this book now, but evaluate the following resources you could use later to hear the message of Christ together.

- An online daily Bible reading plan (e.g., YouVersion, Bible Gateway)

- A daily devotion book (e.g., *Meditations* published by Northwestern Publishing House)

- A daily online devotion (available through many local churches, the Wisconsin Evangelical Lutheran Synod [WELS], and Time of Grace)

- A volume of The People's Bible series

Pray that you continue to find and use a devotional plan so you can hear the message of Jesus together.

Get On the Same Page With Your Finances

Raise your hand if you have a budget. Keep it raised if you stick to it. Keep it raised if you love it. By now, few hands are up. Why is that?

The earth is the LORD's, and everything in it, the world, and all who live in it. PSALM 24:1

We find less in the Bible about family finances and more about our attitudes toward money. But those attitudes, God knows, will shape our family finances. It starts with this: God owns it all. It ends with this: It all goes back to him. Meanwhile, Paul wrote that we can trust him for all we need: "He who did not spare his own Son, but gave him up for us all—how will he not also, along with him, graciously give us all things?" (Romans 8:32). So manage your money like you believe it.

Some will record every penny spent; others won't record anything but will only expend what is allotted. Some will cut up credit cards; others will use only them. What system is best for you? Be suspicious of anyone who tells you one system is godlier than another. Look to financial advisors for help on this. They can help you test-drive different systems and settle on what might work best for you. Then use it.

A pagan or a Christian financial advisor can help, but the Christian who knows his or her field will offer you an advantage: similar attitudes toward money. How you handle your money starts there.

- Have you engaged a financial advisor? Why or why not?

- Write down the questions you would ask a financial advisor. Together, pray about how you might find an answer.

Pray that you are wise in how you're handling God's money.

 **❀ FALL ❀**

Get On the Same Page With Your Finances

We've gotten familiar with the five stages of grief: denial, anger, bargaining, depression, and acceptance. But are you familiar with the five stages of stuff: weaning, gleaning, meaning, cleaning, and leaning? Today: weaning.

**[You have been called] out of darkness
into his wonderful light.** 1 PETER 2:9

When you were baptized into Christ, God called you away from your sinful heart. He gave you a new heart. He daily calls you toward that new heart. God is weaning you because it takes time to live this life. Sometimes sin shows up in our lives and we stop and say, "Wait, that's not me. Why am I thinking like that, talking like that, acting like that?" Those are opportunities for repentance.

Weaning is moving away from your parents and establishing your own home. Is this where you are? Newly married people can be surprised at how hard the adjustment can be. You might have moved to a new area and are weaning yourself from old friends, neighbors, or family. You may have developed financial patterns you'll need to wean yourself from too.

When you were single, financial decisions were less complicated. Your corporation had one stockholder: you. Husbands, chances are you didn't even know a bed needed a skirt. Now you have to spend money on one. Wives, chances are you didn't realize how attached he was to that old chair from his grandma. Now you know.

- If you're newly married, what financial habits might you have to wean away from?

- If you've been married awhile, what financial habits might you still have to wean away from?

Pray that you have the wisdom and strength to leave behind what's no longer helpful in your relationship.

95

Get On the Same Page With Your Finances

We've gotten familiar with the five stages of grief. But are you familiar with the five stages of stuff: weaning, gleaning, meaning, cleaning, and leaning? Today: gleaning.

Let the message of Christ dwell among you richly as you teach and admonish one another. COLOSSIANS 3:16

The Lutheran church is a teaching church. You never know when a person is ready to gobble up the Spirit's words. Parents, your children are also gobbling up, or gleaning, from everyone and everything. Their friends, teachers, and schools will shape their character.

Are you in a phase of also gleaning possessions? Does it feel like you're bringing more into your homes than it can hold? Tools you never needed before fill the garage, a growing arsenal of children's toys (not to mention grown-up toys) poses a trip hazard, and electronics vie for wall outlets. God is lending you some of his money to provide for your family. Don't feel guilty for not spoiling them with everything they want, but do enjoy what brings them joy. Soon enough, your children's toys will be put away or given away, and their closets will be emptied. But that time is not now.

This is usually also the phase in which you're a Pac-Man for learning—gobbling up experiences and information. So make sure you're also gobbling up the truth of God's Word, loving it, pursuing it, and gleaning it.

- These stages aren't necessarily sequential, although they can be. Are you in the gleaning stage, gathering more and more stuff? Tell each other what makes you apprehensive about it and what makes you glad for it.

Pray that you manage your finances while being aware of the stage you're in.

Know Each Other

Marriage can be difficult because there tends to be a negative shift over time. When dating, we look for the positives in the other person and overlook the negatives. But then a shift takes place. About 66 percent of married people say they often feel put down by their spouse.

Whoever seeks good finds favor, but evil comes to one who searches for it. PROVERBS 11:27

You can find things that bother you in anyone. That's easy. People bother you because they're not you. And you worship you. If the human heart is an idol factory, the first idol is self. The funny thing is your spouse can find just as much fault in you for the same reason: We love ourselves.

Only one person lived an idol-free life. Jesus obeyed the First Commandment: "You shall have no other gods" (Exodus 20:3). He didn't live for himself but for the will of God and for you. God knows the negatives about you, but he chooses to look at you through the sinless, selfless nature of his Son.

What do you do that helps you look for the good in your spouse and, better yet, say it? Research shows it takes five positive interactions to heal one negative interaction. Look for the positives. Say them. You can do better than 5:1.

- On your next date, agree that you will have prepared to tell each other, "When we were dating, three of the qualities that attracted me to you were . . ."

- Write down what your spouse tells you. Pray about each one. Ask God to help you strengthen and renew that quality.

Pray that you repent of self-worship, that you accept people the way the Lord accepts you, that you see the good in your spouse, and that you say it.

Know Each Other

The marital satisfaction curve looks like a U. *The honeymoon is on the upper left of the* U *and the 35th anniversary on the upper right of the* U. *Care to guess what's at the bottom? Some research shows happiness increases when the children leave home.*

Children are a heritage from the LORD, offspring a reward from him. PSALM 127:3

Blessings from God, even children, can become distractions. Let's be real: They must distract some attention from your spouse. They have needs, and you need to meet them. Here's the tricky part: You also have needs, and you need to meet them for each other. What's the solution?

Recognize God's blessing. If he gave you children, he entrusted them to you to raise in his paths. But he hasn't asked you to sacrifice your marriage to do so. That would only harm his children. You don't prioritize your children over your relationship with God. So why prioritize them over your marriage?

Your focus on the kids might just be the problem. Express your needs to each other in specific ways. Turn toward each other and not away. Learn a new way to handle conflict. Make your marriage the top priority with confidence that will only benefit your children. The kids will leave; your marriage will remain.

Tell your spouse three specific actions he or she can take to meet each need.

- I need to feel loved (e.g., hold my hand, plan a date, get me coffee, say "I love you," etc.).

- I need to feel respected (e.g., listen to my opinions, be on time, try my suggestion, etc.).

- I need to feel sexy (e.g., kiss me for no reason, touch me like this, etc.).

Pray that you don't make your children the center of your marriage.

❦ FALL ❦

Know Each Other

Mindfulness is another word for "paying attention," "being present," or "concentrating." The Lord God, the Creator of the universe, is mindful of both you and your spouse.

**He tends his flock like a shepherd: He gathers the lambs
in his arms and carries them close to his heart;
he gently leads those that have young.** ISAIAH 40:11

Sheep don't smell nice. Lambs foolishly put themselves in dangerous situations. Yet their shepherd would give his life for them. Likewise, your Good Shepherd has given his life for both of you. After that, doesn't it follow that he would pay attention to you?

How are you doing at paying attention to each other? I know I've not been mindful of my spouse when, before her birthday, I'm in a panic asking my children, "Has Mom mentioned anything she'd like?" For such neglect, I need my Good Shepherd's forgiveness. I may need my wife's forgiveness too.

When does it become painfully apparent to you that you don't know your spouse as well as you'd like? Stop reading and tell each other now.

We can become more mindful. We learn what we want to learn. We find ways to record notes, enter calendar events, or set up reminders. We learn new skills to adapt and flourish when we change jobs or when technology changes. You can apply the same kind of determination to being more mindful of your spouse. Try these or create your own:

- Tell me about your day.

- Let's put a date on the calendar for something special you want to do.

- When and where would it be good for us to create a phone-free zone?

Pray that you give credit to the Good Shepherd who pays attention to you and that you can be more present with your spouse.

❋ FALL ❋

Connect With Each Other

Something is wrong when husbands and wives don't want to be face-to-face. It could be halitosis. Or sin has gotten in the way. Or they just don't know each other.

Jacob called the place Peniel, saying, "It is because I saw God face to face, and yet my life was spared." GENESIS 32:30

When we feel terror in the presence of God, it's because we're aware of our sin. When we find joy and confidence in God's presence, enough to wrestle with him as Jacob did, it's because we know his grace. Jacob knew it was only by God's mercy that he could see his face and live.

When a husband and wife know God's grace, they know they're safe with him. They know his empathy and long to enjoy his presence together.

You want to know your spouse understands what you're feeling or feels a little bit of what you feel. That's empathy. You're more likely to stay in touch with someone who has empathy for you than someone who doesn't have a clue. So here's a conversation to help you see things the way your spouse does and build empathy. It's not a short conversation. It could take place over two or three dates. Don't be afraid to lighten up and laugh at your answers; it's not a root canal.

Couples rarely ask the following questions. Today you will. Listen carefully to your spouse.

- As you look at *your* life, what do you see?

- As you look at *yourself,* what do you see?

- As you look at *me,* what do you see?

- As you look at *us* together, what do you see?

Pray that you find relief in God's kindness and that you find ways to empathize and connect deeply with each other.

Connect With Each Other

Infants begin to focus their eyes at about eight weeks, but they seek out eye contact long before that. There's something about looking into someone's eyes.

The Lord turned and looked straight at Peter. Then Peter remembered the word the Lord had spoken to him: "Before the rooster crows today, you will disown me three times." LUKE 22:61

Peter had been face-to-face with Jesus for three years, but this look was different. He had just denied ever seeing Jesus. Now Jesus' look reminded Peter that Jesus was God, so he knew the future. It reminded Peter of what Peter had just done, but it also reminded Peter of his hope. Jesus didn't turn away from him. The look saddened him (repentance always involves sorrow), but the look kept Peter from despair. It carried him until Jesus looked at him again three days later.

People in love tend to look at each other. The problem is so many other things beg to be seen. Try this experiment. The next time your spouse starts talking to you about the day, the team, the work, the whatever, put your phone away or turn away from your computer. Look at your spouse. Resist the urge to look away. The result might be more than you imagined. Even adults know there's something about looking into another's eyes.

Choose one of these activities:

- Recall together as many details as you can about the surroundings when you first met. Don't stop until you get to ten. Or twenty?

- Tell each other about a time you noticed his or her eye contact. What did it mean to you?

Pray that you trust the Savior's forgiving look and that you can take your eyes off other things to look at your spouse.

✿ FALL ✿

Connect With Each Other

What is it about church that you love? The friends, the music, the pre-dictability, the preaching? David liked the shelter.

**I long to dwell in your tent forever and
take refuge in the shelter of your wings.** PSALM 61:4

The Lord always shelters us with his grace, even outside of the church. But when we gather to hear the Word and receive the Lord's Supper, the Spirit makes us aware of our need for grace. He meets that need at the same time. No wonder we long to be together in church and make time to do it.

People who study relationships advocate for a weekly or biweekly date night. It's worth the time. Reasons for not doing so abound: kids' activities, work, lack of money, being too tired, not having fun together, lack of common interests, etc. Sound familiar? You get creative to solve problems in other areas of your life. You might need to do the same when it comes to date night obstacles.

My wife and I have planned weekly date nights and weekend getaways throughout our marriage. No money? A walk, campfire, or candlelit bubble bath costs nothing. No time? Try 15 minutes sitting outside with a beverage staring at the stars. Don't know how to have fun together? Try something new: Get bikes, take a dance class, check into a hotel with nothing but toothbrushes and an Uber Eats app. You'll figure it out if you want to.

Discuss together:

- Are we making time for each other?

- Agree on two things that interfere with a weekly date night and brainstorm solutions.

Pray that you value the blessings of gathering with the saints in church and the blessings of spending time as just the two of you.

❀ FALL ❀

Enjoy Sexual Intimacy

Getting better at almost anything requires discipline. Why would it be any different with sex?

Husbands, love your wives, just as Christ loved the church and gave himself up for her. In this same way, husbands ought to love their wives as their own bodies. He who loves his wife loves himself. EPHESIANS 5:25,28

Jesus said no to Satan every day of his life. Talk about discipline! We can't come close. Jesus' willingness to give himself up for us is our salvation.

God's plan for you to enjoy his gift of sexual intimacy requires discipline too. Unmarried people may labor under the delusion that once married, it will be nonstop sex. Um, no. A single person who is disciplining sexual desires is practicing for marriage. Married people must discipline those desires when they're apart, sick, traveling, grieving, or just not in the mood. We need to discipline our sexuality after we're married as much as we do before we're married.

God's plan for you to enjoy his gift of sexual intimacy develops discipline too. We learn to discipline ourselves to put the other first. A husband has to discipline himself to slow down to care for his wife. The average man will experience an orgasm in three to seven minutes of sexual play; on average, it takes a woman 20-30 minutes. She may have to discipline herself to be more receptive. He may have to discipline himself to open his heart to her and appreciate that he is about to make love to a person, not just a body.

- Discuss how you've grown in your ability to put the other first when it comes to sex. How would you like to grow?

Pray that you discipline yourself to make sex more enjoyable for your spouse.

❁ FALL ❁

Enjoy Sexual Intimacy

Sex advisors abound. Beware. Unless the opinion you seek comes from the conviction you have about God's plan for marriage, you're on thin ice.

Now that you have purified yourselves by obeying the truth so that you have sincere love for each other, love one another deeply, from the heart. 1 PETER 1:22

Sex is private, sacred, and between a husband and wife. But the practice of biblical sexuality offers blessings that extend far beyond the two of you.

As you practice biblical sexuality, you **give glory to God.** You're giving him credit for the way he's saved you and guided you to live in thankful response.

As you practice biblical sexuality, you **reclaim sex from our culture.** Unfortunately, sexual practices that God calls sinful are considered normal by society. And often, if you don't agree, you'll be accused of being hateful. You may feel like a canary singing in the wilderness, but God can use your voice.

As you practice biblical sexuality, you **cultivate a healthy church.** Men and women, single and married, need each other. The church should be one place where single women can receive attention from godly men who aren't hitting on them, where single men can find mentors who will show them how to treat a wife, and where couples can find others who will walk with them and pray for them.

As you practice biblical sexuality, you **build a healthy family.** Girls know what femininity is because their moms are secure in it themselves. Boys know what masculinity is because they see in their dads a quiet confidence that expresses itself in kindness and self-sacrifice.

- Tell each other about which of the results of practicing biblical sexuality you feel most passionate.

Pray that you bless others through your biblical sexuality.

 **❋ FALL ❋**

Enjoy Sexual Intimacy

Nothing shows the difference between men and women quite like marriage.

How handsome you are, my beloved! Oh, how charming! And our bed is verdant. SONG OF SONGS 1:16

Yeah, but only if we get there. That in itself can be a challenge. What can we do?

Privacy—If you don't have children at home, all you need are window treatments. But if you do, locks on doors are reliable. Turn off the phone. Who needs that intrusion at the wrong moment?

Energy—Why should everything else get our energy? Sometimes work requires almost all we can give, but not always. Sex doesn't always require high energy, but it does require being awake.

Time—Tired sex is not great sex. Start early. Turn off the television. The movie will not be nearly as delightful as your spouse. Declare a social media fast. Leave the files or the laptop at work.

Anticipation—Connect throughout the day. Great sex begins long before clothes come off.

Initiation—Husbands, don't play the dumb game of "I'll see how many days before she initiates." Just initiate. Wives can take on that role too. Past hurts may be real and serious and need to be addressed, but don't let them ruin this important part of your relationship. Work on those things together and start enjoying sex.

Sights and sounds—Maybe that flannel nightgown your mother gave you works for him, but maybe not. And husbands, did you know that husbands who do more housework have better sex lives? The sound of the vacuum may be a powerful aphrodisiac.

- What can we do? What would you add to the list above?

Pray that you enjoy your differences and leverage them to a more enjoyable sex life.

105

 **❀ FALL ❀**

Forgive Each Other

When we need to forgive each other, the distance across the bed can feel like a cavern of space. Sometimes all it takes to begin bridging the gap is an outstretched arm or a touch on the shoulder.

Get rid of all bitterness, rage and anger, brawling and slander, along with every form of malice. Be kind and compassionate to one another, forgiving each other, just as in Christ God forgave you. EPHESIANS 4:31,32

Not everyone knows the last three words of that passage. You do. What an advantage you have! You know that God touched our soil, touched the cross, and now touches you with the good news of forgiveness. He touches you to communicate his love, even when you don't deserve it. You receive it in the absolution, in Baptism, and in his presence in the Lord's Supper.

Our touch can communicate forgiveness too. But what happens when one chooses to hold on to anger and refuses an offered touch? It might look like withdrawing, withholding sex, turning the cold shoulder, or giving abrupt answers or the silent treatment. What then? What does your spouse want then? How could you know?

You could ask. Try it. Tell each other how you would complete the following sentence:

- "When I'm angry, irritated, or withdrawing from you, I wish you would . . ." (Possible answers may be "hug me"; "leave me alone for 30 minutes, then I'll come back"; "ask for my forgiveness specifically by naming what you did"; etc.)

Pray that you can learn to respond to each other in ways that demonstrate love and acceptance.

❋ FALL ❋

Forgive Each Other

I asked the server about "Jordan," the name tattooed on her forearm. "Oh, him," she laughed, "just an old boyfriend, a mistake. I'm married to a wonderful man now." I raised my eyebrows: "What does your husband think about Jordan on your arm?" She smiled, "He doesn't even notice it." Funny what we can do when we resolve to, isn't it?

[Jesus said,] "When you stand praying, if you hold anything against anyone, forgive them, so that your Father in heaven may forgive you your sins." MARK 11:25

Jesus' words tell us forgiveness is more than an emotion. It's resolve. Our sin did not make Jesus feel attracted to us, but his resolve to forgive us moved him to endure the cross, remove our impurity, and call us beautiful in his sight.

To forgive your spouse is not an emotion. It's a choice.

1. When you say, "I forgive you," you're resolving to ask God to bless this person. Who can hold a grudge against someone you're asking God to bless?

2. When you say, "I forgive you," you're letting go of anger. After all, where would you be if the Lord held on to his righteous anger for your sin?

3. When you say, "I forgive you," you're resolving to throw the offense into the deep sea and post a No Fishing sign.

4. When you say, "I forgive you," you're resolving to not bring it up again because love keeps no record of wrongs.

5. When you say, "I forgive you," you're letting go of the right to get even.

- Tell each other, "The statement above that is most like me is . . ." "The one that is the most difficult for me is . . ."

Pray that God strengthens your resolve to forgive because Christ forgave you.

❧ FALL ❧

Forgive Each Other

The TV show M.A.S.H. *made audiences laugh and cry over the horror of war. It's hard to count the number of practical jokes and the times someone said, "I'm sorry," in the almost 300 episodes. But it's easy to count the number of times a character said, "I forgive you." Zero.*

In your love you kept me from the pit of destruction; you have put all my sins behind your back. ISAIAH 38:17

Of all the word pictures the Spirit painted, this must be one of the loveliest. The Lord puts our sins behind his back. Satan and my conscience bring them to the foreground and accuse me. Jesus puts them behind his back and asks Satan, "What sins? I don't see any." Your restoration is complete.

Casually saying "I'm sorry" sends the message "I've done my part. You take it from here." But saying "I need you to forgive me" sends a different message: "I need to end this behavior and put our relationship together again." You're seeking restoration and pledging an active role in pursuing it.

Discuss the following statements. Which apply to you, and which do not? You're seeking to learn how your spouse feels. You may disagree with the reasons, but you can't disagree with the feelings.

- I don't often say, "I'm sorry."

- I tend to say, "I need you to forgive me," rather than "I'm sorry."

- I wish you would ask me to forgive you more often instead of waiting for me to express displeasure.

- I feel you actually forgive me when I ask you to.

Pray that you thank God that he restores and that you learn ways to restore your love through forgiveness.

❧ FALL ❧

Build a Life Together

When you chose a car, the other options didn't go away. How happy would you be if you kept comparing your car to the other possibilities? You're better off taking care of the one you have. But this really isn't about cars.

Guard yourselves in your spirit, and do not act unfaithfully against the wife you married when you were young. He hates divorce! That is what the LORD, the God of Israel, says. MALACHI 2:15,16 (EHV)

God doesn't say he hates divorced people. God loves all people and sent his Son to reconcile sinners to himself regardless of the sin. But that's the point: Divorce for reasons other than unfaithfulness or desertion is a sin and not God's plan for your marriage. So guard yourself in spirit. The Hebrew word for *guard* means "a hedge of protection." Their hedges weren't skimpy, decorative borders. They were impenetrable. How are you doing with building that hedge?

You've heard the expression "the grass is always greener on the other side of the fence." Here are four things you can do to guard against attractive alternatives.

1. **Look for the good parts of your lawn and the weeds in the other lawn.** Every lawn has some parts that are flourishing and some that need work.

2. **Get away from the fence.** I don't have to stand at the fence and look at my neighbor's lawn.

3. **Don't dwell on the greener grass.** Other options haven't left the planet, but you don't have to dwell on them.

4. **Take care of the lawn where you live.** Mature people conclude that even if their spouse isn't perfect, anyone else would simply have different imperfections.

- Discuss actions you can take for each of the four greener grass metaphors.

Pray that you build a strong, protective hedge around your marriage.

Build a Life Together

The only person whose attitudes and actions I have complete control over is me. So why do you suppose when we're not pleased with the way our marriage is going, we try to change the other person?

If it is possible, as far as it depends on you, live at peace with everyone. ROMANS 12:18

"If it is possible." First, we need to admit not all things are possible.

"As far as it depends on you." Second, you can't make your mate into someone he or she isn't. It's your job to love your spouse. It's God's job to make him or her better. You can pray for that, but you are only responsible for the part that depends on you.

"Live at peace." Third, trying to force someone to change is the opposite of promoting peace. If nagging hasn't worked until now, it probably won't in the future. The goal is to build a life together, not to tear it down.

The following exercise can be a game changer. Don't rush it, but don't feel you need hours to do it. It's important to make sure the setting is right: You are both relaxed, not too tired, and able to be honest. Be ready to listen and maybe even take notes. Ask questions to make sure you understand each other. And close with "Thank you."

- Ask your husband, "What things have I said or done that have made you feel respected?"

- Ask your wife, "What things have I said or done that have made you feel loved?"

Pray that you build a life together characterized by love and respect.

❄ FALL ❄

Build a Life Together

If you included a unity candle ceremony in your wedding service, what did you do with the individual candles? Leave them lit? After all, you're still individuals created by the Father, redeemed by the Son, and sanctified by the Spirit. Extinguish them? After all, now you're one. The unity candle came into vogue in the 1970s, mainly at the insistence of mothers—that they might have more of a role in their children's weddings. So what is the right thing to do? We'll never get an answer from the Bible. Maybe this will help.

**Adam and his wife were both naked,
and they felt no shame.** GENESIS 2:25

Right now, the space between you is filled with dust, air pollution, radio waves, microwaves, text messages, and clothes. But there was a time when the first husband and wife had precious little between them . . . literally. The absence of sin meant the absence of lust, fear of being exploited, or just being seen as different. How would you describe how they must have felt walking around naked in the garden and eating fruit? Close, fearless, accepted, open, honest, accessible, free, excited, innocent?

Aren't those the things we want? We won't get them from walking around naked, but we can get them by building a relationship without fear. After all, you weren't drawn to your spouse because you sensed an opportunity for great conflict. Instead, you sensed the possibility of something like Adam and Eve had, not being naked and eating fruit but building a life with a friend.

This is a hard thing to describe, but you and your spouse probably know when you have it and when you don't.

- When have you felt, *This must be what the Garden of Eden was like*? Why?

Pray that you build a love that drives out fear.

❈ FALL ❈

Trust

Recall someone bragging about being patient. You probably can't. We are more likely to brag about experiences or accomplishments. In our culture, patience isn't a virtue. But to dress like Jesus, clothe yourself with patience.

> **As God's chosen people, holy and dearly loved, clothe yourselves with compassion, kindness, humility, gentleness and patience.** COLOSSIANS 3:12

Patience describes Jesus' entire life on earth. The 12-year-old Jesus patiently explained his mission to his parents. After completing his mission, at his ascension, Jesus patiently responded to his disciples' misguided question (Acts 1:6). Patience describes Jesus' orientation toward me too. He forgives my sins not 7 times, not 70 times 7 times, but infinitely. His patience assures me I can trust him.

We need patience to be married as well. You did not marry Jesus Christ. Your husband will not get some things. Your wife won't change some things. Some differences you'll never resolve. Then what? Patience. Kill your pride. Look for the good. Grow in your conviction: *This is the person God intends I live with for the rest of my life.* Recall Jesus' patience with you. One result will be deeper trust.

- Recall two more times in Jesus' life when he showed patience.

- Finish this sentence: "The thing you do that feels most impatient to me is _____ and I wish you'd stop it." Listen to each other, say thank you, and learn from each other. Don't argue or get defensive.

- Tell each other what (or who) is trying your patience right now. Now you know what you can pray about for each other.

Pray with thanksgiving for Jesus' patience with you, and ask him to help your spouse with the thing(s) trying his or her patience.

❈ FALL ❈

Trust

❖

In the traditional marriage vows, we are honest enough to admit there will be times that are "for better" and times that are "for worse." We pray for the former. But the latter, times that are worse, provide even better opportunities to build trust.

**As God's chosen people, holy and dearly loved . . .
bear with each other.** COLOSSIANS 3:12,13

"Bear with each other." Other translations have rendered that as "make allowance for each other's faults" (NLT), "accepting one another" (HCSB), or "put up with each other" (GOD'S WORD Translation). "Just put up with each other" isn't exactly the most romantic description of your marriage, and one hopes it isn't the theme of anyone's marriage, but sometimes . . .

Before Paul was so brutally honest about our need, at times, to put up with each other, he was equally clear about our reason for doing so. You are "God's chosen people." Who chose whom? God chose you. Despite your pain-in-the-neck tendencies, he chose you. He puts up with you for one reason: grace. **G**od's **R**iches **A**t **C**hrist's **E**xpense. And because you've received grace, you can put up with each other.

- Tell each other about one person in your life, other than each other, that you gladly put up with.

- Think of a time your spouse had to put up with you. Yes, just one time! When you're ready, tell each other about that time.

- Why do you think putting up with each other builds trust?

Pray that you remember how often your saving God puts up with you and why. Ask him to help you put up with your spouse when that's needed. Also ask him to help you act in such a way that your spouse not merely puts up with you but instead feels honored by you.

Trust

The modern mindfulness movement invites people to pay attention to their hearts, priorities, and the now. That's not such a bad idea, but the Lord told Jeremiah, "The heart is deceitful above all things and beyond cure" (Jeremiah 17:9). Sounds like we need a better focus for meditation. Try this: Stare back at the One staring at you.

The eyes of the LORD are on those who fear him, on those whose hope is in his unfailing love. PSALM 33:18

The First Commandment nails all of us. Who fears, loves, and trusts God above all things? Not with these hearts we don't. These deceitful hearts are the problem, not the solution. Jesus' perfect heart is our solution. He never failed to fear, love, and trust God above all. His love for you is equally unfailing. He watches over you with perfect mindfulness. Meditate on that. Think about it, ponder it, and recall it throughout the day. Use your Bible, devotion book, phone app, Christian art, or anything that helps you pay attention to the Lord's heart for you.

Your spouse will trust you for two things: your mindfulness of God and your mindfulness of him or her, in that order. Neglect the first, and you could lose your trust in God. Neglect the second, and you could lose your spouse's trust.

- Look around you right now. Name the evidence you see that the Lord never forgets you.

- Look for evidence that you are sometimes *mindless* about your spouse. You don't have to tell each other. This is for your private thinking and repenting.

- Together, determine three things you can each do to be more mindful of the other.

Pray that you are mindful of God's unfailing love by meditating on his Word and that you are more mindful of your spouse.

Pursue Friendship

❖

Everyone loves Jesus' Sermon on the Mount. The problem is no one has ever carried it out except one.

[Jesus said,] "You have heard that it was said to the people long ago, 'You shall not murder, and anyone who murders will be subject to judgment.' But I tell you that anyone who is angry with a brother or sister will be subject to judgment. Again, anyone who says to a brother or sister, 'Raca,' is answerable to the court. And anyone who says, 'You fool!' will be in danger of the fire of hell." MATTHEW 5:21,22

Murder? Never done it. Anger? More problematic. Calling or thinking someone a fool? You're kidding, Jesus, right? He's not. He's showing us how utterly dependent we are on his righteousness. But once received by faith, the Sermon on the Mount becomes a lovely and clear guide. Don't tear down; build up.

When you put down your spouse's thoughts, feelings, or opinions, you're dismantling your friendship. You can disagree without doing that. Another word for it might be *insensitivity.* Let's say one of you enjoys a spirited debate, but the other shuts down at the thought of it. One thinks it's healthy; the other sees it as a put-down. Who needs to change the pattern?

Validations don't do as much good as invalidations do harm. Stopping the negative is more important than doing the positive. You may think you're making up for a put-down by building up the other, but you're in a deep hole.

Want to pursue friendship instead? Accept your spouse's feelings and opinions even if you don't agree. Respect your spouse's character. You married the person, after all.

- Tell each other the last time you felt put down by your spouse, and speak words of forgiveness.

Pray that you build each other up.

❀ FALL ❀

Pursue Friendship

When your spouse walks into the room, and you look up and smile, you've just communicated, "I want to be your friend." It's not much, but these moments added up over time build your friendship.

The heavens declare the glory of God; the skies proclaim the work of his hands. Day after day they pour forth speech; night after night they reveal knowledge. PSALM 19:1,2

The Lord sends us a universe of messages: "I want to be connected to you." You won't find grace in a sunset, an ocean, or the stars, but you will find evidence of the One who loves you to the moon. You do receive grace in the gospel in God's Word and the sacraments.

You can show your spouse your desire for friendship by saying or doing anything that meets his or her needs or wants. They're mostly simple things, like "Can I refill your coffee?" or "Listen to this paragraph." You don't even have to speak. For example, if your favorite food or beverage shows up in the kitchen, you have just received a message: "I want to be your friend."

Then it's your turn to respond. Sometimes a shrug will suffice to let your spouse know you heard. Other times a few words will do it. You can put more energy into it and pursue a conversation about what your spouse did, said, or gave you. Or you can go over the top: "Oh, let me compose a haiku in celebration of our friendship." The point is you turn toward your spouse, literally or figuratively, and send the message: "I want to be your friend too. Thank you."

- Recall something your spouse did or said recently that you took to mean "I want to pursue our friendship."

Pray that you notice when your spouse invites your friendship.

❧ FALL ❧

Pursue Friendship

Was this read at your wedding?

Love is patient, love is kind. It does not envy, it does not boast, it is not proud. It does not dishonor others, it is not self-seeking, it is not easily angered, it keeps no record of wrongs. Love does not delight in evil but rejoices with the truth. It always protects, always trusts, always hopes, always perseveres. 1 CORINTHIANS 13:4-7

In his gospel, the apostle John describes Jesus' actions on the Thursday before Good Friday: "Having loved his own . . . he loved them to the end" (John 13:1). On the cross, you see Jesus act out every description of love in 1 Corinthians 13. There wasn't a self-centered notion in him.

Why are we so often the last to see our own self-centeredness? We could blame our fallen condition, past hurts, indifferent parents, or past failed relationships. When you get married, you are convinced this is the most selfless person you've ever met. A week or two later, though, you begin to conclude this wonderful person has a bit of a self-centered streak. The funny thing is that your spouse is coming to the same conclusion about you at about the same time.

What can you do? You can conclude, "Unless my spouse sees the error of his or her ways, I'm doomed." Or you can treat your own self-centeredness as the problem. Why? Because the only self-centeredness in your marriage you have complete control over is your own. And because "[Jesus] died for all, that those who live should no longer live for themselves but for him who died for them and was raised again" (2 Corinthians 5:15).

- Recall an event in Jesus' life when he demonstrated each description of love in 1 Corinthians 13.

Pray that you admit your self-centeredness and that you grow your friendship with your spouse.

❄ WINTER ❄

Communicate With Each Other

❖

A research article published by the National Academy of Sciences in 2014 showed the average female brain contains more connections between the left and right hemispheres than the average male brain; some say 40 percent more. Our Creator designed husbands and wives to be different.

Love is patient. 1 CORINTHIANS 13:4

Marriage offers plenty of opportunities to be *impatient.* Our God-given neural wiring may account for some of those. Our fallen nature certainly accounts for many. My sinful flesh sets my views as the best, ignores anything that contradicts those views, and then can't understand why my wife won't get on board. Meanwhile, my wife is similarly wondering why and is frustrated that I won't see things her way. Thank God that our Savior saw our greatest need, and instead of being impatient with us, he patiently works repentance and keeps us connected to himself.

In a previous activity, you determined which bridge(s) you wanted to build to better communicate with each other. Here are four helpful hints to keep in mind as you build them.

 1. Be patient. Remember that God has been patient with you.

 2. Be affirming. Our Lord constantly reminds you of your place in his family.

 3. Be helpful. Where would you be without the Holy Spirit's help?

 4. Be grateful. Jesus' patience with you means everything.

Choose one you'll work on today:

- Be patient with your spouse. Give him or her time to formulate thoughts.
- Be affirming to your spouse; try not to correct his or her attempts.
- Be helpful to your spouse, but don't push: "Are you okay with this?"
- Be grateful to your spouse, even for small steps.

Pray that you recall the Lord's patience with you and ask him to help you be patient with your spouse.

Communicate With Each Other

It takes your brain longer to process a negative than a positive. If you tell an employee, "You didn't handle this well," it will take longer to engage in a meaningful way. It may be accurate, but you didn't set the stage for good communication.

**Answer me when I call to you, my righteous God.
Give me relief from my distress;
have mercy on me and hear my prayer.** PSALM 4:1

Our Lord invites two-way communication. We talk to him in prayer; he talks to us in his Word of mercy. We'll never get our part right. We tend to neglect prayer or see it as a way to manipulate God. But Jesus' prayer life was part of his obedience for us. God gives us credit for it. His Word of mercy shapes our conversation with him.

Let his mercy shape your conversations with each other too. Set the stage for good communication. Here are four tips:

1. **Set a positive atmosphere.** Don't jump on your spouse: "You didn't handle that very well." Begin softly, "Can we talk about how that went?"

2. **Be assertive.** Ask for what you want, clearly and respectfully. It's not selfish. It's not the same as demanding. It is letting your spouse know how to serve you.

3. **Listen actively.** Don't interrupt or check your phone. Listen curiously like a friend. Ask questions. Show your spouse you know this is important to him or her.

4. **Respond with understanding.** You may disagree, but you can tell your spouse, "I value you and how you think and feel."

Choose one of the above tips to work on. Tell your spouse which one you're going to focus your attention on.

Pray that you grow to treasure communication with your spouse as you treasure communication with your Lord.

Communicate With Each Other

Do you remember how great it felt to be chosen for a team or how crummy it felt not to be chosen?

> **[Jesus said,] "All things have been committed to me by my Father. No one knows the Son except the Father, and no one knows the Father except the Son and those to whom the Son chooses to reveal him."** MATTHEW 11:27

God has chosen to reveal his Son and your Savior to you. That means he also chose you. Sure, we can hang our heads, aware of how undeserving we are, but we can also lift our heads because God in his grace chose us and revealed himself to us.

Because of God's choice, we can choose things too. We can choose words that hurt or heal: "The words of the reckless pierce like swords, but the tongue of the wise brings healing" (Proverbs 12:18). We can choose sweet words: "Gracious words are a honeycomb, sweet to the soul and healing to the bones" (Proverbs 16:24).

What would your "Communication Commandments" look like? Thou shalt not give the silent treatment? Thou shalt show appreciation? Try to keep an equal number of "thou shalt nots" and "thou shalts." Create your own list privately.

Thou shalt not . . .	Thou shalt . . .
1.	1.
2.	2.
3.	3.
4.	4.
5.	5.

When you're done, compare your Communication Commandments. Tell each other which one you want to work on.

Pray that you show your gratitude for your heavenly Father's choice by the Communication Commandments you choose to follow.

Appreciate Each Other

Have you received a gift because the giver was convinced you'd like it, but you really didn't? It backs you into a corner, doesn't it? Don't tell the giver, and you might receive more of the same; tell the giver, and you might hurt his or her feelings.

Religion that God our Father accepts as pure and faultless is this: to look after orphans and widows in their distress and to keep oneself from being polluted by the world. JAMES 1:27

Hypocrisy says, "I'm religious because I go to church." Saving faith says, "I'm religious because God's gifts of Jesus' forgiveness and repentance move me to look out for the good of others." James tells us to get it right.

Sometimes we get it wrong when we try to show our spouse appreciation. A husband thought his wife loved it when he brought home ice cream. She was trying to avoid it. A wife thought her husband loved trinkets of his favorite musician. He was embarrassed by them. In both cases, their hearts were in the right places, but their actions weren't.

This activity can help you get your hearts and actions to align. Don't blame your spouse for not figuring it out; accept the blame for not telling him or her. You must be honest, or you could end up getting more ice cream or more Merle Haggard T-shirts.

Finish the following sentence. Then prepare to tell each other. You can come back to this again and again, each time finishing the sentence a different way.

- I feel most loved and cared for when you . . .

Pray that you have the right words to tell your spouse what actions you most appreciate.

Appreciate Each Other

❖

Jimmy Fallon wrote a children's book called Your Baby's First Word Will Be DADA. *In his comedic way, he works the word "Dada" into every page. Every new parent longs for that first word and hopes it will be "Dada" or "Mama."*

The Spirit you received does not make you slaves, so that you live in fear again; rather, the Spirit you received brought about your adoption to sonship. And by him we cry, "Abba, Father." ROMANS 8:15

Could you be any more accepted into God's family than that? God the Father allows you to call him "Dada." It wasn't always that way. You were born a slave to Satan, sin, and death. God the Spirit changed that. The Spirit worked faith in you; now you're God's child. Never again do you have to be a slave. You can call God "Father." He loves to hear it.

Your spouse loves to hear your appreciation too. When do you find it most difficult to express it? When you wake up? When you're tired? When you're stressed or busy? You may still appreciate him or her, but it's difficult to communicate it.

The time to find a new job is before you quit your old one. The time to prepare for retirement is before you retire. And the time to plan to express appreciation to your spouse is before you get busy, tired, or stressed. Plan now how you will communicate to your spouse, "How blessed I am that out of all the people in the world, God has chosen you for me!"

- Make a list of five things you will do this week to communicate your appreciation to your spouse. (Don't stop at three or four!)

Pray that you tell your heavenly Father how much you love him and how grateful you are for your spouse.

Appreciate Each Other

A famous hymn gives us a beautiful reminder of our confidence before God: "Just as I am, without one plea but that thy blood was shed for me." Why do you think this has become one of Christianity's most loved hymns? Could it be the relief we get from being accepted by God?

Accept one another, then, just as Christ accepted you, in order to bring praise to God. ROMANS 15:7

God declared us good because of Christ's goodness for us. He only accepts us because of Christ's goodness for us. But because he does, we're able to bring praise to God. That's good!

One way we bring praise to God is by accepting each other. Our culture tries to convince us to accept everyone and everything because morality is unnecessary and nonexistent. Just accept everyone. Embrace sin. The gospel convinces us to accept everyone not because of their goodness but because of what Jesus has done for all. Accept everyone by calling all to repent of sin. That's how the Spirit makes more disciples who bring praise to God.

You went to the altar because you saw good in each other. Over time, though, it's easy to forget that. Opposites attract; then they repel. We can go from being our spouse's good-finder to being our spouse's fault-finder without knowing it. The antidote? "Accept one another."

- Recall the good things that attracted you to your spouse in the first place. Include strengths that he or she has that you lack. You can also discuss a time one of your spouse's strengths helped you through a difficult time or task. If you're ready now, tell each other. If not, set a time when you will.

Pray that you praise God for his acceptance of you and that you find ways to accept your spouse.

Manage Conflict

Everyone has good habits and bad habits. Before you continue, tell each other one good habit you notice in your spouse. We'll get to the bad later.

On the Sabbath day [Jesus] went into the synagogue, as was his custom. LUKE 4:16

Jesus was sinless; so were his habits. He never offended his Father. His habits were only good. His followers? Not so much. But Jesus was in the habit of obeying his Father and loving his neighbor precisely because we don't.

Unlike Jesus, we pick up bad habits along with the good, and they don't serve us well. When you were single, a bad habit like not making the bed didn't bother anyone (unless your mother came to visit). But now every bad habit has the potential to make any conflict worse. If you don't make the bed (or whatever chore is yours to do) when you have a conflict, it is like throwing fuel on a fire.

What habits do you have that fuel the fires of conflict in your marriage? Here's a list. Tell each other, "One of my bad habits that could fuel the fire of conflict in our marriage is . . ." Please note, you're going to tell each other your own bad habit, not the other's bad habit. Take your time. Prepare. Then tell your spouse and listen to your spouse. You don't have to agree or disagree, but you might thank your spouse for opening up to you.

Yelling	Physical contact
Raising voice	Negative body language
Clamming up	Getting in the other's face
Pushing the issue	Bringing up the past
Repeating self	Getting overly emotional
Sarcasm	Belittling
Have to have the last word	"You always . . ./You never . . ."

Pray for motivation and strength to change any bad habits.

Manage Conflict

Anger isn't sinful; Jesus got angry. What you do next, though, will either glorify God or sin against him.

[Jesus] looked around at them in anger and, deeply distressed at their stubborn hearts, said to the man, "Stretch out your hand." He stretched it out, and his hand was completely restored. MARK 3:5

What angered Jesus was obvious: people rejecting him, the very people he was in the act of saving. Notice Jesus' response. Even in his anger, he loved. He healed the man and showed the crowd how mistaken they were to reject him. He gave them another chance to see that he's the Son of God.

Our anger can be helpful. Anger is a natural response to a threat. But what if the anger itself is the threat? What if your anger threatens your marriage? You could suppress it; you could put on a happy face. That doesn't sound healthy. You could hold on to it, remember it, and rehearse it. That sounds spiritually and physically harmful. You could become cynical, sarcastic, and critical. That sounds like it would make you very hard to live with. Or you could become aware that you're getting angry and decide in advance what to do with it.

- Think through which caution flags you experience when you become angry. Here's a list of common options:
  - Jaw clenches
  - Heart races
  - Face flushes
  - Stomach feels sick
  - Fists clench
  - Muscles tighten
  - Breathing changes
  - Vocal pitch/tone changes

- Tell each other which caution flags you experience when you're becoming angry. Listen to your spouse and learn from her or him.

Pray that you use your anger against sin and Satan, not your spouse.

Manage Conflict

When parents see their faults in their children, they wince. Parents wince frequently.

Who can discern their own errors?
Forgive my hidden faults. PSALM 19:12

Even those blessed to have been raised by godly parents have to admit we got the bad with the good. In Baptism, though, the worst we received from our parents was washed away. The guilt of the sin handed down to us is gone, but the fallen nature remains. Some of our "hidden faults" may trace back to our parents, including how we handle conflict. We don't need to be ashamed of it, but we gain much by understanding it.

When it comes to managing conflict, we often live what we learned. Our past experiences tend to shape our present actions. These questions will help you explore what you learned about managing conflict when you were growing up. Handle this with grace and sensitivity. You didn't have perfect parents—nothing new there. This isn't about bashing them but about understanding how we got to where we are now and plotting a course for the future.

1. How did I handle conflict with my parents?
2. What did my parents do right in resolving conflict with each other?
3. What did my parents do wrong in resolving conflict with each other?
4. What have been my tendencies in dealing with conflict with friends?
5. If someone was watching us deal with a conflict, what would you want him or her to see?
6. What skills or habits would help you deal with conflict in the future?

Pray that you learn from your parents' examples, both what to imitate and what not to imitate.

Serve Each Other

Think of one gift your spouse has given you that, if your home were on fire, you might run in to retrieve. Another of Dr. Chapman's love languages is Receiving Gifts.

God so loved the world that he gave his one and only Son, that whoever believes in him shall not perish but have eternal life. JOHN 3:16

God is a giver. He gave the law so we would know our need for a Savior. He gave his Son so we would be his children. In addition, he gives every earthly blessing for our enjoyment, including marriage.

Does your spouse feel loved by receiving gifts? For some, a gift is a visual demonstration of love. Gifts mean more to some than to others. One spouse lights up like a Christmas tree when receiving a gift; another might be calmly grateful. For those who feel loved by receiving gifts, the cost doesn't seem to matter. Pardon the cliché, but it really is the thought that counts.

Some gifts you hold in your hands, like the one from the opening paragraph. Tell each other why you'd risk your life to retrieve it.

The gift of yourself is a different kind of gift but is just as powerful. It means being there when your spouse needs you to share a laugh, do a job, or just listen. Being there speaks loudly to the one whose primary language is receiving gifts.

What would you say to a husband/wife, not your own, who tells you:

- My spouse loves golf more than me.

- I can't recall giving my spouse a gift other than on special occasions.

- My spouse is going way overboard with gifts.

Pray that you better appreciate God's gifts to you and better understand how your spouse feels about gifts.

Serve Each Other

"I know my spouse loves me. The house is clean, meals are prepared, and the kids are cared for." You wonder if the person was referring to a maid, a chef, or a nanny. But don't be too quick to judge. It could also be a spouse whose primary love language is the fourth of Dr. Chapman's love languages: Acts of Service.

Read the following verses and tell each other your observations about Jesus' acts of service.

> **You see, at just the right time, when we were still powerless, Christ died for the ungodly. Very rarely will anyone die for a righteous person, though for a good person someone might possibly dare to die. But God demonstrates his own love for us in this: While we were still sinners, Christ died for us.** ROMANS 5:6-8

Jesus served in ways only he could. He served regardless of our unworthiness. Did you note the timing? "While we were still sinners . . ." Christ's death shows his total commitment. We don't replicate Jesus' actions, but we can learn from him.

My father showered gifts on my mother. I learned that's what husbands do. But my wife didn't respond to my gifts by weeping like Miss America. She was grateful, but her primary love language is acts of service. Washing the windows makes her feel more loved than a gift. Vacuuming the carpet, according to her, is one of the sexiest things I do. Does your spouse feel loved by your acts of service?

- Your parents' marriage was theirs. Yours is yours. Discuss your parents' influence on how you show your love to your spouse and what you might want to change.

Pray that you do the acts of service that make your spouse feel loved.

Serve Each Other

❖

A fifth love language, according to Dr. Gary Chapman, is Physical Touch. Does your spouse feel love from you by your touch?

Jesus had compassion on them and touched their eyes. Immediately they received their sight and followed him. MATTHEW 20:34

Why do you think Jesus so often touched the people he healed? He didn't have to. His words had the power to heal. But he touched. He knew sin alienated us from God and from each other. He came to reconcile us to both. He touched people to show his love and to show how we can love.

You can spot a spouse who feels loved by physical touch. It's the couple holding hands, sitting on the same side of the booth, or maybe he has his arm around her shoulders in church. You can't tell if both feel that way. One spouse may not, but he or she is touching for the same reason Jesus did: to show love.

Determine if your spouse feels love from your touch by finishing these sentences.

- The ideal length of time for a back massage is . . .

- They were outlawed in junior high, but now when it comes to PDA (public displays of affection), would you like *(a)* more, *(b)* less, or *(c)* about the same?

- On a scale of 1 (low) to 10 (high), the "touching" factor in my childhood home was . . .

- Your hug means more to me than your words when . . .

- Tell each other which one or two languages best communicate love to you: words of affirmation, quality time, receiving gifts, acts of service, or physical touch.

Pray that you respond joyfully and speak willingly your spouse's love language.

Spiritual Intimacy

The busier Martin Luther got, the more he considered he needed time in prayer. He didn't consider prayer a waste of time. Neither did Jesus.

Very early in the morning, while it was still dark, Jesus got up, left the house and went off to a solitary place, where he prayed. MARK 1:35

Prayer and Bible study go together. God speaks to us through his Word. We speak to God in prayer. Both are necessary. Luther likely didn't sit for three hours with his head bowed and hands folded. Rather, he had his Bible open and dialogued with God as he studied it.

Praying together builds spiritual intimacy. I know of a family that closes its devotion with a written prayer, and then each person, from youngest to oldest, adds a sentence or two. Prayer is speaking to God, and being able to listen to someone else's prayer tells us what is on his or her heart.

If you're uncomfortable praying aloud, use a written prayer and add your own thought to it. Written prayers are helpful, but they may not include what's on your mind. The editors of this book decided not to include fully written prayers for each devotion. Instead, the prayer guide is intended to help you. Begin simply, "Dear God," and use the guide from there. Whether using prayers written by others or speaking prayers directly from your heart, praying together will build your spiritual intimacy.

Which of these suggestions might you try?

- After turning the lights out, hold hands and thank God for the blessings of the day.

- At breakfast, say a brief prayer of protection for each family member.

- Include the Lord's Prayer or Luther's Morning or Evening Prayer.

- Close your family devotions with children adding their prayers.

Pray that you make a habit of praying together.

Spiritual Intimacy

What thought occupies your mind most often? How about this?

**See what great love the Father has lavished on us,
that we should be called children of God!
And that is what we are!** 1 JOHN 3:1

John takes you to the cross to see God lavishing his love on you. It took nothing less than the death of God's own Son for you to be called "children of God." Spiritual intimacy begins there. See the price Jesus paid for your sin and be amazed by God's love.

Not everyone is a child of God. Jesus turned to some religious leaders and said, "You are not children of God. You're children of your father, the devil, and I see the family resemblance" (see John 8:42-47). Everyone is either a child of God through faith in Christ or a child of the devil. You and your spouse are children of God by the miracle of rebirth into Christ.

The King James Version begins the 1 John verse with "Behold!" How many problems in your marriage would be leveled by *beholding* that God has made you his children? Are you upset right now because your spouse doesn't see something your way? You're *beholding* that instead of this. Are you worried that God may not let your life go the way you want? You're *beholding* that instead of this. The more clearly you behold the lavishness of God's adoptive love, the better you'll handle every storm that comes your way.

- Family meeting agenda: What can we do to remind ourselves, "We are children of God by faith in Christ. We want to behold God's love for us"? What's getting in the way? How can we help each other *behold* this joyful truth?

Pray that you behold the lavish love of God for you and your spouse daily.

Spiritual Intimacy

You may not often use the term covenant *in your day-to-day life, but God calls your marriage a covenant.*

She is your partner, the wife of your marriage covenant.
MALACHI 2:14

A *covenant* is a solemn agreement to put the good of the relationship ahead of your individual desires. God describes his love for you as a covenant: his solemn promise to act in love for you. When Jesus was about to shed his blood on the cross, he called it the "blood of the covenant" shed for you (Matthew 26:28). Occasionally, Scripture describes a two-way agreement—you do this, and God will do that. Those never worked out because people would fail. God's covenant of forgiveness does work out because it's one-sided. It only depends on God. And he's perfectly faithful.

Only once does God directly call marriage a covenant, but he describes it as a covenant throughout the Bible. When you married, you made an agreement with God and with each other to put the good of your relationship ahead of your immediate needs or wants.

The value of a covenant is that it stays the same even when circumstances change. Think of how many of your circumstances have changed since you were first married. You both have and will change in ways you never could have imagined on your wedding day. The challenge and delight of marriage are to act in ways that demonstrate your covenant even as things change.

- See how your covenant endures through changes: Tell your spouse three ways you're not the same person you were on your wedding day.

- Tell your spouse, "Two things you do to show me you put our marriage before yourself are . . ."

Pray that you keep your covenant. Regardless of changes in your lives, you will be the one who will always be there.

Get On the Same Page With Your Finances

You've heard of the five stages of stuff: weaning, gleaning, meaning, cleaning, and leaning. Today: meaning.

**We are God's handiwork, created in Christ Jesus
to do good works, which God prepared
in advance for us to do.** EPHESIANS 2:10

This is the time when you're humming. You're learning what to say no to and what to say yes to. It's a moving target, but you make decisions not just to gather more stuff or to have more experiences but to pursue what you're convinced is the reason God gave you life and called you into his kingdom. You're asking, "God, why am I here?"

To put it positively, "God, what is the good work you've prepared for me to do?" To put it negatively, "God, show me what I'm spending my time or money on that is at best foolish and at worst sinful."

If you don't have children, you can bounce answers off each other. If God gives you children, you can teach them the importance of meaning, even in finances. A child in one family asked his parents, "You guys make enough money. Why don't we have a nice car instead of keeping these old cars running?" The parents calmly asked him to add up the amount they were giving to the work of their church and for his and his siblings' Christian education. He did the math. End of discussion. It may not be easy to teach a child what's meaningful in your family, but it's priceless, and no one else can do it for you.

- Tell each other what you spend money on that makes you feel the best or most fulfilled.

Pray that you bless others and build the kingdom of God with your time and money.

Get On the Same Page With Your Finances

You've heard of the five stages of stuff: weaning, gleaning, meaning, cleaning, and leaning. Today: cleaning. Jesus' disciples asked him about the future. He replied:

"It is not for you to know the times or dates the Father has set by his own authority." ACTS 1:7

In other words, "You know me. You know what I've done for the world. That's enough."

Don't let God's grace for one season of life become an idol for the next season of life. God may have given you health, an income level, a big house, and even adult kids nearby for one season of life. Don't make of his blessings for one season of life an idol in the next. You know Jesus. You know what he's done for you. That's enough for your future.

Constant cleaning is necessary. The half-life of information is so quick that many resource books are outdated before they gather dust on your shelf. But it isn't just books.

Chances are some things you once knew about your spouse are no longer true. He or she has changed. Clean out those old ideas. Maybe you picked up a spending habit that is no longer necessary. Clean it out. Maybe God gave you a material blessing in one season of life he isn't giving you in your current season of life. Let it go.

This phase hits harder as we get older. But imagine how much lighter you may feel if you learn to do it now.

- Think of possessions or financial assets you have that you don't need and could benefit others. What's keeping you from blessing others with them?

Pray that you trust God for the future and clean out what you don't need.

Get On the Same Page With Your Finances

You've heard of the five stages of stuff: weaning, gleaning, meaning, cleaning, and leaning. Today: leaning. The last stage of life is where you began. But when you began, leaning was natural; at the end, you must learn it.

Remember your Creator in the days of your youth, before the days of trouble come and the years approach when you will say, "I find no pleasure in them." The dust returns to the ground it came from, and the spirit returns to God who gave it. ECCLESIASTES 12:1,7

As we age, we learn to lean on each other in new ways. We learn anew what was true throughout our marriages: We need each other.

If you're leaning on your spouse right now, no need to apologize. You are giving your spouse the chance to live a dignified life, caring for someone other than self. Leaning on each other allows you to live out the second table of God's law: "Love your neighbor as yourself" (Matthew 19:19). I'd say your spouse should thank you, but let's not push it.

Jesus lived through each stage of life. He weaned himself from his parents' home and his familiar job. He gleaned knowledge of God's Word so that he could use it to benefit others. He pursued meaning, knowing he had come to live and die for you. He cleaned out his life—by the time he died, he literally had nothing. And he leaned: "Father, into your hands I commit my spirit" (Luke 23:46). The result was resurrection. Your resurrection. Jesus lived every stage of his life for you.

- Think of an elderly married couple you know. Ask the couple how they've managed changes in finances throughout their marriage.

Pray that you are filled with Jesus' truth, changed by him, and used in his plan to save others.

Know Each Other

It's easy to avoid the unpleasant. Doctors and dentists schedule your next appointment for you because you might not do it. It's easy to avoid potentially unpleasant conversations with each other too.

**A gentle answer turns away wrath,
but a harsh word stirs up anger.** PROVERBS 15:1

Jesus had every reason to be harsh with his disciples, but he seldom was. His usual way was gentleness. Jesus bore the harshness they deserved. In turn, they received the patience, kindness, and gentleness of God. You've received the same.

Sometimes getting to know each other means treading lightly on sensitive ground. One of you may have gotten your way at the expense of the other's dream. One of you may feel hurt from the past or, just as troubling, uncertainty about the future. Of course it's best to discuss such things when the mood is good, but who wants to spoil a good mood?

How can you have that conversation and not spoil the good mood?

- Pray. Ask your Savior to fill you with his gentleness. Clarify what you want out of this conversation.

- Prepare to get defensive and avoid it. When you want to lash out, tell yourself you knew that inclination was coming. Knowing this enemy will help you defeat it. Your spouse will face the same enemy. You can't defeat it for him or her.

- Don't belittle yourself or your concern. If it's gotten to this point, it's not silly, and you may not be able to just stop thinking about it.

- Use the language of self-disclosure: "I feel . . ."

- Don't press for a solution. Even if you don't resolve the thing, you've grown to know each other better. That's a win.

Pray that you can be gentle, even in a difficult conversation.

Know Each Other

Do you find yourselves finishing each other's sentences? Congratulations. You have an awareness of each other to build upon. How will you do it?

"Let the one who boasts boast about this: that they have the understanding to know me, that I am the Lord, who exercises kindness, justice and righteousness on earth, for in these I delight," declares the Lord. JEREMIAH 9:24

You began to know God at your baptism, but Jesus didn't want your knowledge of God to end there. He followed up the command to baptize with the command to teach his Word. Through God's Word you have come to know him better: his kindness toward sinners, his justice satisfied in Christ, and his righteousness given to you. Know his Word, and you can finish God's sentences. That's something to boast about.

You can build on your knowledge of your spouse too. But unlike the unchanging God, your spouse is always changing. Your spouse may have changed a goal for the future or even dropped a dream. With outdated knowledge, you won't be able to serve your spouse the way Christ has served you. How do you keep your knowledge bank updated?

- Try to recall the first question you ever asked your spouse or your spouse asked you. Imagine you were to meet today for the first time and ask the same questions. Tell each other your updated answer.

- Try finishing each other's sentence:

  ○ "Do you remember where I left my . . ."

  ○ "I think it's time we . . ."

  ○ "Before we get too old to do it, I think we should . . ."

Pray that you grow in your knowledge of God and your knowledge of each other.

Know Each Other

It's best for dating couples to dial down physical passion and pursue deep friendship. It's best for married couples to pursue both.

"In that day," declares the LORD, "you will call me 'my husband'; you will no longer call me 'my master.' I will betroth you to me forever; I will betroth you in righteousness and justice, in love and compassion." HOSEA 2:16,19

Why would God use that kind of language to help us know him? Because he doesn't want us to relate to him in fear but in love. His loyalty to us elicits curiosity; we want to know him better. We're never done exploring God.

And we're never done getting to know each other better. God wants to use your marriage as a signpost, pointing others to him. That happens best as you're getting to know him and each other better.

Take turns asking each other these questions. Don't rush it. Listen and explore. You can always come back to the ones you don't get to today:

- What was one of your favorite childhood memories?

- Which two living people do you most admire?

- What is your favorite time for making love?

- What is one of your favorite books, other than the Bible?

- What is your least favorite household task?

- What would you like me to pray about for you?

- What would you say would be an ideal way to spend an evening?

Pray that you continue to ask each other questions to better know each other.

Connect With Each Other

❖

Lack of companionship is a frequently cited reason for divorce. In other words, at least in one spouse's opinion, they stopped connecting with each other.

Submit to one another out of reverence for Christ.
EPHESIANS 5:21

What? Only a dog submits. What if you changed the word to "be willing to allow something to go someone else's way instead of insisting on your own way"? It's cumbersome but also more accurate. It's what the Son of God did for you, not because you're superior to him but because he chose to. It's what you can do for your spouse without a hint of who's superior or inferior.

One counselor suggests, "If one of you enjoys a recreational activity that bothers the other or cannot include the other, it must be dropped." That's a strong statement. Argue against it if you wish, but don't dismiss it too quickly. Some of our best feelings occur when we're pursuing our favorite recreation. Is it wise to share them with anyone other than your spouse? You decide.

Maybe you'll decide a girly girl can don a motorcycle helmet and ride on the back of a Harley. A manly man can shuffle through quilt patterns at the fabric store. The husband who can't play a tune can usher for his wife's recital. A woman who fears the water can sail while wearing a life jacket. Recreational activities come in all shapes, but they touch our emotions. When you find a way to enjoy them (or at least do them) together, you'll connect with each other.

- Brainstorm ten recreational activities you might possibly enjoy doing together. Mark three you would most enjoy doing with your spouse. Compare your lists.

Pray that you put the other first, even when it comes to choices of recreation.

❄ WINTER ❄

Connect With Each Other

❖

Have you read a book that seemed too short? Good conversations are like that.

[Jesus said,] "Listen carefully to what I am about to tell you: The Son of Man is going to be delivered into the hands of men." LUKE 9:44

"Listen carefully" seems like an odd thing for Jesus to say. Isn't everything he said important? Isn't the whole Bible God's Word? Yes, but some things matter more. Jesus told a man he healed to go back home. It was good for the man and good for those in his home. But here Jesus was telling his disciples about his impending arrest and execution. This would be good for them and every human. Nothing matters more.

Some conversations must be mundane: "Who's picking up Joey from practice? Did you put gas in the car? When will you be home?" Some conversations are more revealing: opinions on medical needs, beliefs about the economy, and where to vacation. Even deeper conversations often begin with "I'm sad . . . I'm glad . . . I'm mad . . ." You don't have to live there. But to connect with each other, you must get there occasionally.

Undoubtedly one of you is less talkative than the other. If that's you, only you can conclude if the reason is laziness or nature. Listening for meaning and thoughtfully responding takes work, but it's work that matters.

Here are some ways to bring more meaningful conversation into your life. Think of more and try the ones that appeal to you.

- Look into each other's eyes until one of you laughs. It will help you communicate.
- Throughout the day, jot on a notecard the things you want to talk about.
- Take notes in church and compare them later.
- Plan a quarterly "Vision for the Future" meeting with just the two of you.

Pray that you have the courage to have important conversations.

Connect With Each Other

What do you think of when you hear the expression bonding time? A parent playing with a child? Glue drying? Jesus thought of your marriage.

What God has joined together, let no one separate. MARK 10:9

The second half of that verse gets plenty of play in Christian circles. But don't neglect the first half. You didn't choose each other as much as God chose you for each other. There's nothing admirable in thinking you're so sufficient you don't need your spouse. On the contrary, you need each other to be the person God has called you to be. Praying together, worshiping together, and receiving the Lord's Supper together are all ways you can tighten your three-way bond: the two of you and Jesus.

What bonds a couple? One cancels a meeting or takes off work to be there when the other receives an award. When one is testy or grouchy, the other quietly sits nearby, waiting for the right time to touch or whisper encouragement. One grabs the other's hand to pray while waiting for a message about test results, a loved one, or a job. One goes with the other even to an event or concert that isn't his or her style. One grabs the Bible or devotion book and reads to the other after a meal or before bed.

- Recall an activity you once enjoyed doing together and try it again.

- When you were dating, something pulled you along and kept you together. Remind each other what that was and discuss how it can still tighten your bond.

Pray that you see your spouse as God's choice for you and that you pursue activities that tighten your bond.

Enjoy Sexual Intimacy

When was the last time you prayed for your sex life? Get ready.

**This is my prayer: that your love may abound more
and more in knowledge and depth of insight, so that
you may be able to discern what is best and may be
pure and blameless for the day of Christ, filled with
the fruit of righteousness that comes through Jesus Christ—
to the glory and praise of God.** PHILIPPIANS 1:9-11

Paul's prayer is beautiful, eloquent, and inspired by God. Our prayers may be lacking in comparison, but that's not the point. Your heavenly Father invites you to bring your prayers to him on any subject, and that even includes your sex life.

Just a note of caution about what you pray for. Hollywood and culture will regularly redefine beauty. Today's preferred shape will give way to another. In ancient India, the Sanskrit word for a beautiful woman is *gajagamini*. It means "a woman who has the gait of an elephant." We can't ask our spouse to meet the world's ever-changing beauty standards. Instead, ask God to help you define beauty by your spouse's body and nothing else.

What you fantasize over will shape what you desire. Why not make that your spouse? Ask God to shape your desires so you're attracted only to your spouse.

- Write a prayer for your sex life. Be specific! For example, describe what you're grateful for, pray specifically for what you want, and thank God for your spouse. Some starters might be: Thank you, Lord, for . . . Help us to see . . . Teach us how to serve one another by . . .

Pray the prayer that you've written.

Enjoy Sexual Intimacy

Where do people get the idea that God is a cosmic killjoy? God created sex. He isn't interested in making our lives boring.

The husband should fulfill his marital duty to his wife, and likewise the wife to her husband. The wife does not have authority over her own body but yields it to her husband. In the same way, the husband does not have authority over his own body but yields it to his wife. Do not deprive each other except perhaps by mutual consent and for a time, so that you may devote yourselves to prayer. 1 CORINTHIANS 7:3-5

You both have rights over each other's bodies. Each has the right to lay claim to the other's body for sexual intimacy. But Paul doesn't say, "So stake your claim. Get your rights." He says, "Husband, give her the rights that belong to her," and "Wives, give him the rights that belong to him." It's a selfless giving rather than a selfish taking.

He also says, "Do not deprive each other." He's not encouraging either of you to seize sexual gratification whenever you want without regard for the other, but he's urging both of you to be ready to give your body when the other wants it.

The point is you, not me. Your enjoyment of sexual intimacy depends on each of you trying to satisfy the other. Husbands, do so with understanding. Your tender words at 7 A.M. might be what she needs to want to make love to you at 10 P.M. Wives, he may want sex more than you do. It's wrong for him to take what you won't give, but it's possible for you to give even when the time doesn't feel ideal.

- The ideal number of times per week for us to have sexual relations is . . .

Pray that you maintain a generous spirit about sexual intimacy.

Enjoy Sexual Intimacy

Your physical relationship is more vulnerable to the effects of worry, anger, and tension than any other area. They are foxes seeking to ruin the vineyard of physical intimacy.

**My dove in the clefts of the rock, . . . show me your face,
let me hear your voice; for your voice is sweet, and
your face is lovely. Catch for us the foxes,
the little foxes that ruin the vineyards,
our vineyards that are in bloom.** SONG OF SONGS 2:14,15

The garden and fruit are images of love and passion. The little foxes are things that ruin both.

What are the little foxes that nip at your physical oneness? One may be conflict. The little day-to-day conflicts build barriers. Christ's forgiving love for both of you tears them down. In the peace of forgiveness, agree to have time together when you keep talk of problems off-limits. You can pick them up again later, but don't let them ruin your vineyard.

Another little fox may be neglecting the importance of sensuality to your sexuality. Sex is what you do in bed (and other places); sensuality is a consequence of being human and includes an array of preferences. Did you pay more attention to senses when you were dating? Now perhaps you're more likely to get right to the main event. You might benefit from backing up a bit. Nonsexual sensuality is a big part of what leads to sexuality.

Another little fox may be anxiety. Worry about making a mistake, how you look, hygiene, the kids walking in, etc., can be barriers to enjoying sex. Get creative about solutions. Talk about them. Laugh about them. And kick that fox out of your vineyard.

- Agree on two little foxes that are sometimes ruining your vineyard. What will you do about them?

Pray that Christ's promise to you moves you to follow through and catch the foxes.

Forgive Each Other

❖

Quick: Name those three magic relationship words. I don't mean "Let's have tacos" or "Here's your coffee." I don't even mean "I love you." Three other words stand as tall: "I forgive you."

God was reconciling the world to himself in Christ, not counting people's sins against them. 2 CORINTHIANS 5:19

Paul went on to say that God has committed to us the message of reconciliation. *To us.* All brothers and sisters in Christ have the ministry of announcing to one another, "Your sins are forgiven." Why don't we? In church, we call a pastor to exercise this public ministry of reconciliation on our behalf, but privately, we can and must announce reconciliation. In marriage, we do so primarily when we announce, "I forgive you." But what holds us back?

Is it pride? We all have it, but confessing our own sin to God makes it easier to forgive when we've been wronged.

Is it self-righteousness? That's like watching a professional play a sport and correcting him or her from the couch. The reality is we are all equally fallen, and although Satan may tempt us differently, each of us is capable of horrendous sin.

Is it because we want to punish the other just a little? Or maybe a lot? After all, how else will our spouse know the error of his or her ways? And, by the way, Lord, I'd like to have a hand in determining the punishment.

Discuss the danger in the following statements.

- "I forgive you, but I'm sick and tired of forgiving you for the same thing."

- "I'll forgive you—this time."

- "I'll forgive you if you promise not to make the same mistake again."

Pray that you learn to forgive as you have been forgiven.

Forgive Each Other

❖

In what area are you seeking growth? Your golf game, passport stamps, or job? How about growing in your ability to forgive? That takes grace.

He does not treat us as our sins deserve or repay us according to our iniquities. For as high as the heavens are above the earth, so great is his love for those who fear him; as far as the east is from the west, so far has he removed our transgressions from us. PSALM 103:10-12

Grace is a gift and a growth. The gift comes with faith through Baptism. Growth comes as the Holy Spirit continues to transform us into the image of Christ, day by day. Christ's image is grace, love for the unlovable. When we see the price he paid for our sin, we grow in grace.

Don't be shocked when, after you forgive your spouse, a thought of revenge surfaces. For us, unlike for God, grace is a growth process. Peter wrote, "Grow in the grace and knowledge of our Lord and Savior Jesus Christ" (2 Peter 3:18). Such growth only happens as we encounter God's grace in the gospel.

Which of the following passages would you consider painting on a wall in your home?

1. "He does not treat us as our sins deserve or repay us according to our iniquities" (Psalm 103:10).

2. "As far as the east is from the west, so far has he removed our transgressions from us" (Psalm 103:12).

3. "Be kind and compassionate to one another, forgiving each other, just as in Christ God forgave you" (Ephesians 4:32).

4. "Bear with each other and forgive one another if any of you has a grievance against someone. Forgive as the Lord forgave you" (Colossians 3:13).

Pray that you are filled with God's grace to forgive.

Forgive Each Other

Some have called the church the fellowship of the forgiven. It's a good name for your marriage too.

Forgive us our debts, as we also have forgiven our debtors.
MATTHEW 6:12

Our world is a mess. Our families can get messy. It's obvious we live a million miles from heaven. None of us would want a transcript of our every conversation posted publicly, much less a podcast of all our thoughts about each other. One conduit flows from heaven to earth and connects us to God and each other: forgiveness. It's really the only way to keep both of those relationships alive.

After teaching this prayer, Jesus revisited this petition and explained, "If you forgive other people when they sin against you, your heavenly Father will also forgive you. But if you do not forgive others their sins, your Father will not forgive your sins" (Matthew 6:14,15). This petition isn't just about God's action; it's also about our own willingness to live in forgiveness.

No magic pill can heal all marriage wounds, but this is close. Forgiveness mends our spats, reconciles us when we're separated, calms us when we're angry, and opens our arms to receive each other. No magic can do that; forgiving grace can.

- Each day for the next six weeks, include one of the seven petitions of the Lord's Prayer in your daily prayers. A catechism can help you mine the words for rich meaning. Discuss with each other what you're learning.

- The next time you're worshiping together, join hands during the Lord's Prayer. Jesus doesn't mind, others might learn from it, and you might apply the prayer in a fresh way.

Pray that you find renewed meaning for your marriage in the Lord's Prayer.

Build a Life Together

❖

Law enforcement professionals are expected to de-escalate tense situations. Learn to do the same in your marriage to build a life together.

The words of the reckless pierce like swords, but the tongue of the wise brings healing. PROVERBS 12:18

Satan doesn't want you to build a life together. He'd rather you speak reckless words than wise words. But you have two very big things in your favor: Jesus has crushed Satan's head and, as Paul wrote, "we are not unaware of his schemes" (2 Corinthians 2:11).

Some factors that often negatively affect marriage are out of your control: your parents divorced; you were young when you got married; you lived together first; you had different faith backgrounds, poor financial means, or personality disorders. By the way, if any of those describe you, aren't you glad God's grace has made you an exception?

Now is the time you can control. Your marriage is about how you think and act now. When you sense tension escalating, getting bigger like a snowball rolling downhill, or one of you is upping the ante, you're more likely to speak reckless words. Whether you're yelling or subtly attacking, the problem is you can never get those words back.

So what can you do? Pray for wisdom. Ask yourself, *What would bring healing?* You can back off, soften your tone, lower your defenses, restate your spouse's view, turn the talk another way, and clearly display humility.

- Which practices in the preceding paragraph have you mastered? Which ones need some work?

Pray that you receive sweet words from Jesus and learn to speak sweetly to each other.

Build a Life Together

You've seen mission statements at church, work, and the convenience store. What's your marriage mission statement?

[Joshua said,] "Choose for yourselves this day whom you will serve. . . . As for me and my household, we will serve the LORD." JOSHUA 24:15

In Joshua 24:14-24, you'll encounter the word *serve* 11 times. The Israelites had often wandered from following the Lord. Now they had settled in the land the Lord had given them. Joshua was leading them to create a mission statement to reflect their gratitude. It's worth the effort to create your family's mission statement.

First, make a list of fundamental values—things important to your marriage. You might include laughter, fun, shared faith, family, meals together, hard work, exercise. Then cross off things that you'd like but aren't reality. Cross off things everyone likes such as truthfulness, honesty, etc.

Second, write down an extensive list of facts about your family. These are things that help you make decisions week by week and month by month. For example, you might write how many children you have or want, where you live, if you are into gardening, no pets, etc. This can get messy, but don't let that stop you. Just write.

Third, of all that you wrote for the second step, agree on the three most important items.

Finally, use your first list and your top-three list to write one paragraph, two to four sentences, to describe how your marriage and family are unique. "We are a family that values . . . We are a family that does . . ." Congratulations. You've created your mission statement!

- Post your mission statement on your refrigerator, talk about it, and refine it.

- Describe the Israelites' reasons for wanting to serve the Lord and how they could show they served the Lord.

Pray that you serve the Lord together.

Build a Life Together

When you got married, you told your friends what you had in common: "We love the same team, music, etc." You began building your life together around that. But that can change. Maybe you change allegiance to a team or change your mind about what you like to do. Then what?

We proclaim to you what we have seen and heard, so that you also may have fellowship with us. And our fellowship is with the Father and with his Son, Jesus Christ. 1 JOHN 1:3

Jesus calls you his friend and creates a deeper kind of friendship among us. Sin gets in the way. There's anger and hurt even among Christians. But Jesus credits his sinless life to your account and takes away the sin that separates you from God and each other. The whole point of life now becomes friendship with God and each other.

Your spouse is about to tell you some of the deepest and most private parts of his or her life. The intelligent spouse will listen, learn, and ask questions: "What do you mean? Can you give me an example? Tell me more." That's how you build your life together. The not-so-intelligent spouse will question, argue, or belittle with "I just haven't seen that in you at all." Will you be the intelligent or the not-so-intelligent spouse?

If your time is too limited now, plan when you will tell each other:

- What am I trying to accomplish with my life?

- What is my dream?

- What do I see as God's purpose for my life?

- How do I want to be remembered when I'm gone?

- What changes might I make in our relationship to accomplish some of these?

Pray that you build on your fellowship with Christ.

❄ WINTER ❄

Trust

Would you pay attention if a financial advisor told you a strategy that would increase the likelihood of funding your retirement? Probably. What if there were a strategy that would dramatically increase the likelihood that you'll not only still be married to each other six years from now, but you'll also be happy together? Would you be interested? Absolutely. Here's part one of that strategy.

**The LORD bless you and keep you . . .
the LORD turn his face toward you.** NUMBERS 6:24,26

The Lord told Moses this was how he was to bless the people. They often turned away from him, but blessing and hope would come from this: "the LORD turn his face toward you." We call that grace.

How do you turn your face to each other? Let me start the list: bring home your spouse's favorite food, text to say you'll be late, rub his or her shoulders, or pray for each other. Watch for your spouse expressing, usually unspoken, "I want to be connected to you." Then respond intentionally. Here's the first and best way to respond: turn *toward* your spouse. Acknowledge that he or she has just done something to communicate, "I want to be connected to you." Your response might require little energy ("Thanks") or more energy (asking questions). Notice your spouse indicating, "I want to be connected to you." Then show you noticed: turn toward your spouse.

- Tell each other two ways your spouse has expressed, "I want to be connected to *you*."

- Brainstorm five ways you can turn toward your spouse when you notice his or her expression, "I want to be connected to you."

Pray that you would notice your spouse saying, "I want to be connected to you," and that you turn toward your spouse when you do.

151

Trust

❖

Part one: Catch your spouse doing something that says, "I want to be connected to you," and turn toward your spouse. Part two: Catch your spouse doing something that says, "I want to be connected to you," and don't "turn against" your spouse.

Even my close friend, someone I trusted, one who shared my bread, has turned against me. PSALM 41:9

Many psalms are messianic because they describe Jesus. These words describe Judas betraying Jesus. These words also describe the betrayal King David felt when advisors and family turned against him. You've felt it too when a friend turned against you. It's hard to trust after that.

When you catch your spouse doing or saying something that communicates, "I want to be connected to you," and you respond by finding fault ("You didn't put the dishes away correctly") or by arguing about a detail ("Always use the touchless car wash, never the brush kind") or by criticizing ("What's wrong with you? Can't you do anything right?"), you're killing trust. Listen carefully to what you say. When you catch yourself turning against your spouse, stop talking. Talk to Jesus. Confess your sin. Thank him for not turning against you and giving you trust in him. Ask him to help you turn toward, not against, your spouse.

- Eavesdrop on the following conversations. Write how each spouse might respond in two different ways.
  She says in the grocery store aisle, "Are we out of dish soap?"
  He says (turning toward):
  He says (turning against):

  He says while driving, "Isn't that boat like the one we saw on vacation last year?"
  She says (turning toward):
  She says (turning against):

- In your opinion, why does turning against kill trust?

Pray that you repent of turning against your spouse and that you make a habit of turning *toward* him or her.

Trust

Part three: Catch your spouse doing something that says, "I want to be connected to you," and don't "turn away" from him or her.

Do not hide your face from me, do not turn your servant away in anger; you have been my helper. Do not reject me or forsake me, God my Savior. PSALM 27:9

Do you hear the desperation in David's prayer? He knew if the Lord turned away from him, he'd have no helper. But David calls God his Savior, his helper in the most important way. By the Savior's help alone we have life with God. Aren't you glad he doesn't turn away from us?

Wives, in Genesis 2:18, the Lord reveals his plan for marriage. Be your husband's "helper" (same Hebrew word as Psalm 27:9). What an honor you have! Be a picture for your husband of the Lord's help for us; don't turn away from him.

Husbands, in Genesis 2:24, the Lord reveals his plan for marriage. Be united to your wife and don't turn away from her. What an honor you have! Be a picture for your wife of the trust she can have in God her Savior.

- Turning away is different from turning against. It's more like apathy. Determine why apathy could be worse than turning against each other.

- Think for a minute about how you will complete the following sentence. Then tell each other. "One way I have turned away from you is . . . and I'm sorry. Please forgive me."

Pray that the Lord does not turn his face away from you but that you see his grace through his Word and sacrament. Confess the times you've turned away from your spouse, and ask God to help you replace that with turning toward him or her.

Pursue Friendship

❖

The Japanese martial arts philosophy of aikido *is to yield to win. To oppose brute force with brute force is a mistake. You must yield to win.*

Do not let any unwholesome talk come out of your mouths, but only what is helpful for building others up according to their needs, that it may benefit those who listen. EPHESIANS 4:29

When you accept influence from your spouse, you build him or her up. You show love and respect. You demonstrate your reverence for Christ by putting the other first. You glorify God for all to see. And when what you do and say benefits your spouse, it also benefits you.

You're never more likely to influence someone else than when you have accepted influence from that person. And if you needed more incentive, some say the higher a married couple rates their friendship, the higher they rate their sex life.

Your willingness to accept influence helps you be fully present and give your full attention to your spouse before offering your point of view. Do you see how this would help you manage a conflict? The knee-jerk reaction isn't to get defensive. Your goal isn't to get your spouse to see it your way but to understand how he or she thinks. That's how friends act.

This activity may take some time to think about before you do it. You might set a time tomorrow when you'll do it.

- Tell your spouse, "One way you've influenced me for good is . . ."

Pray that you learn to accept influence from your spouse to better serve him or her and pursue your friendship.

Pursue Friendship

Jim Carrey starred in Liar Liar, *a movie about a father who let down his son one too many times. The son wished his father could only tell the truth and got his wish. That's the plot. It's a comedy because, well, to only tell the truth is laughable.*

Each of you must put off falsehood and speak truthfully to your neighbor, for we are all members of one body. EPHESIANS 4:25

When Adam and Eve fell into sin, the Lord didn't become a stone wall to them. Instead, he entered their world, promised them a Savior, and kept them from eating of the tree and being separated from him forever. Thank God he still tells us the truth! "The wages of sin is death, but the gift of God is eternal life in Christ Jesus our Lord" (Romans 6:23). We don't like the first part, but we love the second. The truth is we need both.

Equally as harmful as not speaking the truth is not speaking at all. You won't pursue friendship if you don't carry on that important discussion. If you shut down, get quiet, or look away, you stonewall. Stonewalling is the opposite of pursuing friendship.

If God made you more like a rock in the desert than a babbling brook, that's a strength. Don't let your strength become a weakness. You can speak. If you don't, your friendship will decline. If you don't, you'll be giving the impression you're independent of your spouse, and that's not true. If you're the talker, stop nagging. It won't help. If you're the stonewaller, learn a new dance. You can.

- If you're the stonewaller, tell your spouse what might coax you into speaking more to build your friendship.

Pray that you speak the truth in love.

❄ WINTER ❄

Pursue Friendship

❖

Your friendship is a renewable resource. Whether things are good or bad, now is the best time to cultivate that relationship.

[Jesus said,] "I am the vine; you are the branches. If you remain in me and I in you, you will bear much fruit; apart from me you can do nothing." JOHN 15:5

The essence of marriage is your promise to live as husband and wife until death. Keeping that promise is a fruit of your faith. Since faith comes from the message of Christ, your friendship will too. It really is all about Jesus. When there's a problem in your friendship, you don't just have a marriage problem. You have a Jesus problem. Grow in Jesus through his Word and the sacraments.

A dream marriage doesn't mean both husband and wife are perfect and never hurt each other. Instead, a dream marriage is filled with forgiving, serving, communicating, enduring in trials, and enjoying emotional, spiritual, and physical connections to the end. That's your dream.

Cheer each other on. When you complain or argue, it's devastating. When you don't encourage, it's as if you're jeering, not cheering. As one couple put it, "Even when you're in conflict, you honor each other. That's what being a cheerleader is about."

Someone cheering you on from the sidelines can be a powerful motivator. Cheerleaders stick around even after the fans are gone and the game looks hopeless. Cheerleaders stay to the end. And they come back for the next game.

- What cheers us on might be different. Since your spouse is the best marriage teacher you have, ask each other, "What can I do to cheer you on?"

- When it comes to reading the Bible, praying together, worshiping in church, participating in a Bible study, or receiving the Lord's Supper, I wish we could . . .

Pray that you become each other's cheerleader.